SHAPE UP YOUR LANGUAGE

An Introduction to Basic Language Structures
PART I: Verbs—Past Tense

by Joan M. Frazer and Cynthia J. Smith
illustrated by Vincenza Genovese

**Communication
Skill Builders**
3130 N. Dodge Blvd./P.O. Box 42050
Tucson, Arizona 85733
(602) 323-7500

Mimeographing

If you prefer to copy the designated reproducible materials by mimeographing and you have access to a thermal copier, you can easily make your own mimeograph stencils. It is not necessary to tear pages out of this book. Make a photocopy of the desired page. Use this photocopy to make a stencil on a thermal copier.

© 1983 by

**Communication
Skill Builders, Inc.** ®
3130 N. Dodge Blvd./P.O. Box 42050
Tucson, Arizona 85733
(602) 323-7500

ISBN 0-88450-828-5   Catalog No. 7024

10 9 8 7 6 5 4 3 2

Printed in the United States of America

About the Authors

Joan M. Frazer holds a B.A. from the University of Michigan and an M.A. from Arizona State University. She also holds the C.C.C. In Speech from the American Speech–Language–Hearing Association.

In addition to her work as a Speech–Language Pathologist in Phoenix, Arizona, Ms. Frazer is a founder of Communication Skill Builders and has co-authored several educational products published by CSB.

Cynthia J. Smith completed her undergraduate work in Communication Disorders and Audiology. She holds an M.S. in Speech Pathology from Arizona State University. Ms. Smith has worked with speech- and language-impaired preschoolers and the hearing impaired. She is presently employed as a Speech Clinician in Colorado Springs, Colorado.

Other products by Joan M. Frazer and Cynthia J. Smith and available from Communication Skill Builders:

Shape Up Your Language
  Part II: Nouns — Plurals (1983)
  Part III: Adjectives — Comparatives and Superlatives (1983)
Shape Up Your Language — A Complete Kit (1983)

Other products by Joan M. Frazer and available from Communication Skill Builders:

With Valeda Blockcolsky, Barbara Kurn, and Elizabeth Metz
  Peel 'n Put Speech and Language Programs (1968-77)
  Gameboards for Speech and Language Development (1976)
With Valeda D. Blockcolsky
  Star Trails (1978, 1980)
With Valeda D. Blockcolsky and Douglas H. Frazer
  30,000 Selected Words (1979)

Contents

Shape Up Your Verbs 1

Section 1 5

walk   pull   paint
push   open   hunt
hop   close   point
talk   climb   add

Section 2 71

find   break   sleep
eat   drink   feed
sit   shake   sweep
take   wear   bring

Section 3 139

sing   run   make
study   ring   shoot
give   strike   write
draw   ride   buy

Section 4 207

fall   dig   swing
catch   fly   slide
throw   blow   hide
build   swim   hang

Flashcards 275

Shape Up Your Verbs

Shape Up Your Language, Part I: Verbs — Past Tense presents a lively format for teaching children the past tense of 48 regular and irregular verbs. Fun-filled activities introduce grammatical concepts and help children to integrate them into spontaneous language.

These materials may be used successfully with speech- and hearing-impaired children, with children learning English as a second language, and with normally speaking children.

The Materials

This volume of *Shape Up Your Language* includes the following:
- Reproducible pre/post-test sheets
- Reproducible basic worksheets, review worksheets, activity pages, summary worksheets, and progress charts
- Reproducible flashcard pages
- Instructions for using the program

Sources

It is recommended that the teacher/speech pathologist review the grammatical concepts to be taught. Two suggested sources are:

Jespersen, Otto. *Essentials of English Grammar.* University,
    AL: University of Alabama Press, 1964.

Palmer, F. R. *The English Verb.* London: Longman Group
    Limited, 1974.

How to Use These Materials

1. *Part I: Verbs — Past Tense* consists of four sections. Begin with Section 1 or choose a section that is most pertinent to student needs.
2. Make a copy of the appropriate pre/post-test sheet for each student.
3. Make flashcards by reproducing the flashcard pages (located at the end of each section) and cutting them apart inside the black lines. For greater durability, laminate the cards or paste them on card stock.
4. Show the student the picture side of flashcard **1a.** Say, "This picture shows *is walking.* The bear *is walking.*" Then show the picture side of flashcard **1b** and ask, "What did the bear do?"

    The first answer may be modeled so the student will understand what kind of answer is expected. If the student responds correctly, put a check in the *correct* column on the pre-test side of the test sheet. If the response is incorrect, put a check in the *incorrect* column. Repeat with all the flashcards for that section. Begin administering the program if the student has more than two incorrect responses.

5. Make copies of the appropriate worksheets, reviews, and summaries for each student. Assign one worksheet, review, or summary at a time. Ask the students to write their names and the date in the blanks provided.
6. As the students complete the worksheets, give assistance as needed. Let non-reading students respond orally while you write their responses on the worksheets.
7. Review the completed worksheets, reviews, and summaries with the students and explain the answers. Let each student put a check in the box after each response and record the number of completed answers at the end of the worksheet section.
8. Copy the progress chart for the section the student is working on. Write the student's name and the date in the blanks provided. Tally the results on the progress chart.
9. Students will receive further reinforcement by doing the activity sheets following each set of worksheets.
10. When one section is completed, use the pre/post-test sheet to administer the post-test. When 85% or more of the responses are correct, the section is successfully completed. The minimum number of correct answers necessary to complete the section appears at the bottom of each pre/post-test sheet. **Do not proceed to the next section until the post-test goal has been met.**

Branching and Reinforcement
Evaluate the results on the progress chart periodically to follow the student's progress.

   If an area of weakness is identified, review and reinforce that area by using the flashcards. They may be used in group activities, with one student at a time, and at home.

A Complete Kit

In addition to this volume, a complete kit for *Shape Up Your Language* has been developed. It includes:

1. *Part I: Verbs — Past Tense* (48 verbs)
2. *Part II: Nouns — Plurals* (40 nouns)
3. *Part III: Adjectives — Comparatives and Superlatives* (20 adjectives)
4. Reproducible flashcard pages (236 flashcards)
5. Three acrylic shapes for manipulation and matching structures
6. 59 picture-and-word strips for inserting into the acrylic shapes
7. Comprehensive Instructional Manual

The complete *Shape Up Your Language* kit is available from Communication Skill Builders, P. O. Box 42050, Tucson, Arizona 85733 (602) 323-7500.

Shape Up Your Language

Part I: Verbs — Past Tense

Section 1

Pre/Post-Test Sheet 1 6
walked (1a/b) Worksheet 1 7
              Activity Sheet 1 10
pushed (2a/b) Worksheet 2 11
              Activity Sheet 2 14
hopped (3a/b) Worksheet 3 15
              Activity Sheet 3 18
talked (4a/b) Worksheet 4 19
              Activity Sheet 4 22
Review 1 23

pulled (5a/b) Worksheet 5 25
              Activity Sheet 5 28
opened (6a/b) Worksheet 6 29
              Activity Sheet 6 32
closed (7a/b) Worksheet 7 33
              Activity Sheet 7 36
climbed (8a/b) Worksheet 8 37
              Activity Sheet 8 40
Review 2 41

painted (9a/b) Worksheet 9 43
               Activity Sheet 9 46
hunted (10a/b) Worksheet 10 47
               Activity Sheet 10 50
pointed (11a/b) Worksheet 11 51
               Activity Sheet 11 54
added (12a/b)   Worksheet 12 55
               Activity Sheet 12 59
Review 3 60

Picture Summary 1 62
Game 1: Mix and Match 64
Summary Worksheet 1: Writing Sentences 65
Summary Worksheet 2: The Tree House 67
Progress Chart 1 69

Name: _____

Pre/Post-Test Sheet (Verbs: Section 1)

Make flashcards of pictures 1a/b through 12a/b. See page 1 of manual.

Pre-Test	Date: _____	correct	incorrect	Post-Test	Date: _____	correct	incorrect
1	walked			1	walked		
2	pushed			2	pushed		
3	hopped			3	hopped		
4	talked			4	talked		
5	pulled			5	pulled		
6	opened			6	opened		
7	closed			7	closed		
8	climbed			8	climbed		
9	painted			9	painted		
10	hunted			10	hunted		
11	pointed			11	pointed		
12	added			12	added		

Post-Test Objective: The student will achieve 85% accuracy (10 out of 12 words). Repeat entire section if objective is not met.

Verbs: Section 1
Pre/Post-Test Sheet 1

Name: _____ **Date:** _____

◯

△

is walking

walked

1. **Find the picture that matches.**
   Fill in the blank with the correct word:

◯ The bear is walking down the path.

△ The bear _____ down the path.

walk

walked

2. **Write and say:**

walked

_____

– – – – – – – – – – – – – – – – –

_____

Verbs: Section 1
Worksheet 1-1 (walked)

3. Fill in and say:

Yesterday my sister and I _____
to school.

4. Answer the question. Write your sentence in the blank:

When did you walk to a friend's house?

_____
- -
=======================================
- -

5. Fill in the missing letters and say the word:

walked

walke __

walk __ __

wal __ __ __

wa __ __ __ __

w __ __ __ __ __

__ __ __ __ __ __

Verbs: Section 1
Worksheet 1-2 (walked)

6. Write and say the word four times:

walked

- - - - - - - - - - - - - - -
═══════════════════════════
- - - - - - - - - - - - - - -
───────────────────────────
- - - - - - - - - - - - - - -
───────────────────────────
- - - - - - - - - - - - - - -
───────────────────────────

**7. Study the two words below.
    Then close your eyes and spell:**

walk

walked

**Put a 1 in each little box for your answer.
Add up your answers.
Write the total in this big box.**

Verbs: Section 1
Worksheet 1-3 (walked)

Name: _____ **Date:** _____

Find the path the boy walked home on.

1. How did the boy get home?
2. Show me and tell me which way he walked.

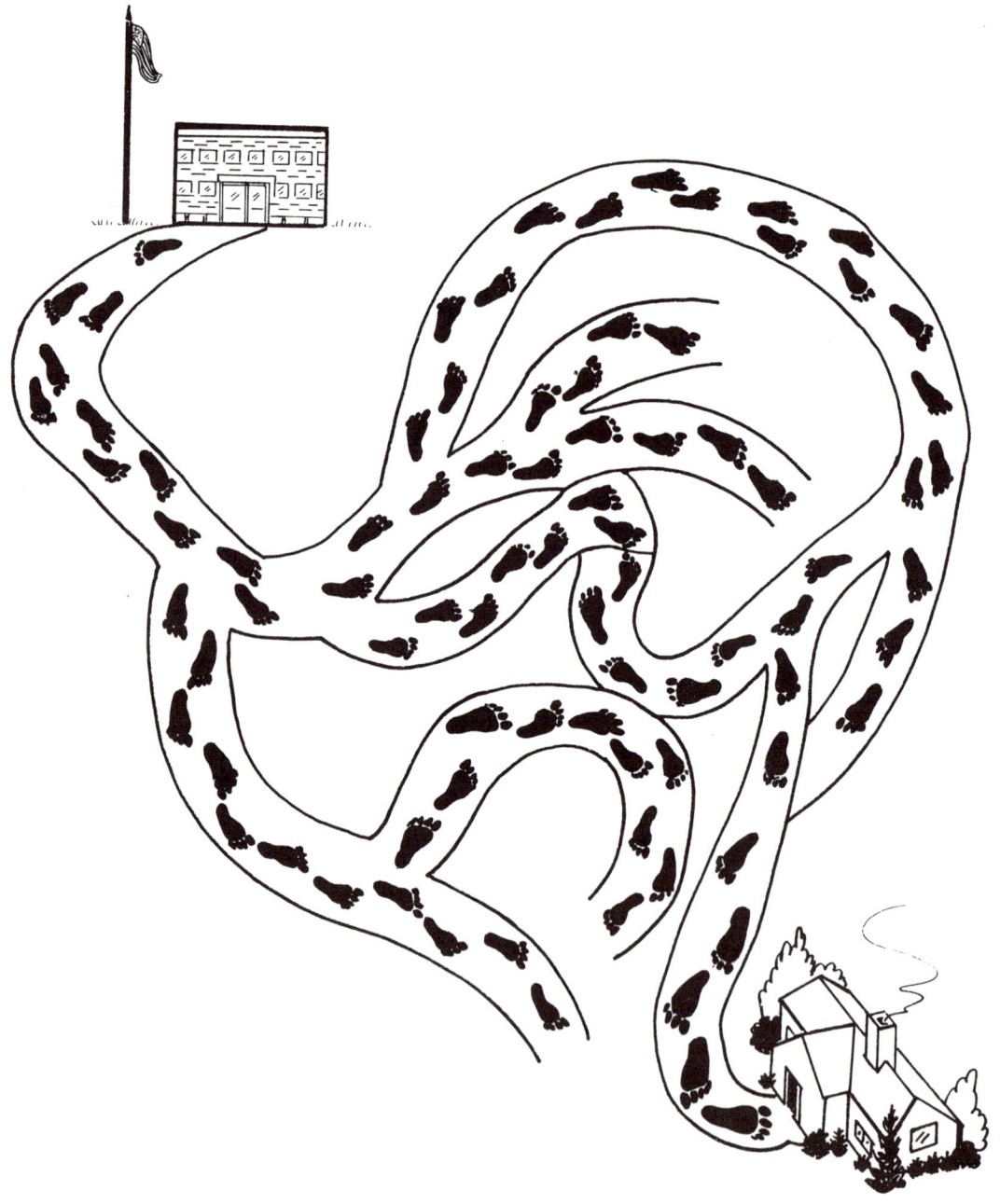

Verbs: Section 1
Activity Sheet 1 (walked)

○

△

is pushing

pushed

1. **Find the picture that matches.**
   Fill in the blank with the correct word:

○ The bear is pushing the car.

△ The bear _____ the car.

pushed

push

2. **Write and say:**

pushed

_____

_ _ _ _ _ _ _ _ _ _ _ _ _

_____

Verbs: Section 1
Worksheet 2-1 (pushed)

3. Fill in and say:

Yesterday he _____ the bike across the street.

☐

4. Answer the question. Write your sentence in the blank:

Why did he push the bike across the street?

☐

_____

\- \- \- \- \- \- \- \- \- \- \- \- \- \- \- \- \- \- \-

_____

\- \- \- \- \- \- \- \- \- \- \- \- \- \- \- \- \- \- \-

_____

5. Fill in the missing letters and say the word:

☐

pushed

pushe __

push __ __

pus __ __ __

pu __ __ __ __

p __ __ __ __ __

__ __ __ __ __ __

Verbs: Section 1
Worksheet 2-2 (pushed)

6. Write and say the word four times:

pushed

7. Study the two words below.
Then close your eyes and spell:

push

pushed

Put a 1 in each little box for your answer.
Add up your answers.
Write the total in this big box.

Verbs: Section 1
Worksheet 2-3 (pushed)

Name: _____ **Date:** _____

Draw a lawn mower for the man to push.

1. What is the man pushing?
2. What did he do yesterday?
3. Did you ever push a lawn mower? Tell about it.

Verbs: Section 1
Activity Sheet 2 (pushed)

Name: _____ **Date:** _____

is hopping    hopped

1. **Find the picture that matches.**
    Fill in the blank with the correct word:

⃝ The kangaroo is hopping.

△ The kangaroo _____.

hopped

hop

2. **Write and say:**

hopped

_____

‑ ‑ ‑ ‑ ‑ ‑ ‑ ‑ ‑ ‑ ‑ ‑ ‑ ‑ ‑

_____

Verbs: Section 1
Worksheet 3-1 (hopped)

3. Fill in and say:

Yesterday the girl _____ over the fence.

4. Answer the question. Write your sentence in the blank:

When did you hop over something?

_____

— — — — — — — — — — — — — — — — — — — —

_____

— — — — — — — — — — — — — — — — — — — —

_____

5. Fill in the missing letters and say the word:

hopped

hoppe —

hopp — —

hop — — —

ho — — — —

h — — — — —

— — — — — —

Verbs: Section 1
Worksheet 3-2 (hopped)

6. Write and say the word four times:

hopped

_____

— — — — — — — — — — — — —

_____
_____

— — — — — — — — — — — — —

_____

— — — — — — — — — — — — —

— — — — — — — — — — — — —

7. Study the two words below.
Then close your eyes and spell:

hop

hopped

Put a 1 in each little box for your answer.
Add up your answers.
Write the total in this big box.

Name: _____ **Date:** _____

Color and cut out the rabbit.
Make the rabbit hop on the table.

1. **What is the rabbit doing?**
2. **What did the rabbit do?**

Verbs: Section 1
Activity Sheet 3 (hopped)

Name: _____   **Date:** _____

○

△

is talking   talked

1. **Find the picture that matches.**
   Fill in the blank with the correct word:

○ The rabbit is talking on the phone.

△ The rabbit _____ on the phone.

   talked

   talk

2. **Write and say:**

   talked

   _____

   _ _ _ _ _ _ _ _ _ _ _ _ _ _ _ _ _

   _____

Verbs: Section 1
Worksheet 4-1 (talked)

3. Fill in and say:

Yesterday the teacher _____ about the story.

4. Answer the question. Write your sentence in the blank:

When did you talk on the phone?

_____

– – – – – – – – – – – – – – – – – – – –

_____

– – – – – – – – – – – – – – – – – – – –

_____

5. Fill in the missing letters and say the word:

talked

talke __

talk __ __

tal __ __ __

ta __ __ __ __

t __ __ __ __ __

__ __ __ __ __ __

Verbs: Section 1
Worksheet 4-2 (talked)

6. Write and say the word four times:

talked

7. Study the two words below.
Then close your eyes and spell:

talk

talked

Put a 1 in each little box for your answer.
Add up your answers.
Write the total in this big box.

Verbs: Section 1
Worksheet 4-3 (talked)

Name: _____ **Date:** _____

Color and cut out the telephone.

Punch out holes in telephone and receiver.
Attach telephone to receiver with yarn.
Call someone and talk.

1. What are you doing?
2. Who did you talk to?

Name: _____ **Date:** _____

Fill in the blank with the correct word.
Then say the complete sentence:

1. Today the kangaroo is hopping.

   Yesterday the kangaroo _____.

   hop
   hopped
   □

2. Yesterday the bear walked to the store.

   Today the bear _____ to the store.

   is walking
   walk
   □

3. Today the bear is pushing the car.

   Yesterday the bear _____ the car.

   push
   pushed
   □

4. Yesterday the rabbit talked on the phone.

   Today the rabbit _____ on the phone.

   talk
   is talking
   □

23

5. Today the bear is walking to the store.

Yesterday the bear _____ to the store.

walk
walked

☐

6. Yesterday the bear pushed the car.

Today the bear _____ the car.

is pushing
push

☐

7. Today the rabbit is talking on the phone.

Yesterday the rabbit _____ on the phone.

talked
talk

☐

8. Yesterday the kangaroo hopped.

Today the kangaroo _____.

is hopping
hop

☐

Put a 1 in each little box for your answer.
Add up your answers.
Write the total in this big box.

Name: _____ **Date:** _____

○ △

are pulling   pulled

1. **Find the picture that matches.**
   Fill in the blank with the correct word:

○ The pigs are pulling the rope.

△ The pigs _____ the rope.

pulled

pull

2. **Write and say:**

pulled

_____

_ _ _ _ _ _ _ _ _ _ _ _ _ _ _ _

_____

Verbs: Section 1
Worksheet 5-1 (pulled)

3. Fill in and say:

Yesterday we _____ the weeds
in the garden.

4. Answer the question. Write your sentence in the blank:

Did you ever pull a wagon?

_____
 _ _ _ _ _ _ _ _ _ _ _ _ _ _ _ _ _ _
_____
_____
 _ _ _ _ _ _ _ _ _ _ _ _ _ _ _ _ _ _
_____

5. Fill in the missing letters and say the word:

pulled

pulle _

pull _ _

pul _ _ _

pu _ _ _ _

p _ _ _ _ _

 _ _ _ _ _ _

Verbs: Section 1
Worksheet 5-2 (pulled)

6. Write and say the word four times:

pulled

‾‾‾‾‾‾‾‾‾‾‾‾‾‾‾‾‾‾‾‾‾‾‾‾‾‾

– – – – – – – – – – – – – –

‾‾‾‾‾‾‾‾‾‾‾‾‾‾‾‾‾‾‾‾‾‾‾‾‾‾

– – – – – – – – – – – – – –

‾‾‾‾‾‾‾‾‾‾‾‾‾‾‾‾‾‾‾‾‾‾‾‾‾‾

– – – – – – – – – – – – – –

‾‾‾‾‾‾‾‾‾‾‾‾‾‾‾‾‾‾‾‾‾‾‾‾‾‾

– – – – – – – – – – – – – –

7. Study the two words below.
Then close your eyes and spell:

pull

pulled

Put a 1 in each little box for your answer.
Add up your answers.
Write the total in this big box.

Verbs: Section 1
Worksheet 5-3 (pulled)

Draw a wagon for the boy to pull.

1. **What is he doing?**
2. **Tell a story about pulling a wagon to your friend's house.**

Verbs: Section 1
Activity Sheet 5 (pulled)

Name: _____   **Date:** _____

◯

△

is opening   opened

1. Find the picture that matches.
   Fill in the blank with the correct word:

◯ The rabbit is opening the door.

△ The rabbit _____ the door.

opened

open

2. Write and say:

opened

_____

_ _ _ _ _ _ _ _ _ _ _ _ _

_____

Verbs: Section 1
Worksheet 6-1 (opened)

3. Fill in and say:

Yesterday I _____ the gate.

4. Answer the question. Write your sentence in the blank:

How many presents did you open on your birthday?

_____

- -

_____

- -

_____

5. Fill in the missing letters and say the word:

opened

opene __

open __ __

ope __ __ __

op __ __ __ __

o __ __ __ __ __

__ __ __ __ __ __

Verbs: Section 1
Worksheet 6-2 (opened)

6. Write and say the word four times:

opened

**7. Study the two words below.
Then close your eyes and spell:**

open

opened

**Put a 1 in each little box for your answer.
Add up your answers.
Write the total in this big box.**

Verbs: Section 1
Worksheet 6-3 (opened)

Cut along the dark line.
Fold the door open along the dotted line.
Open the door.

1. **What are you doing?**
2. **What did you do?**
3. **What else did you open today?**

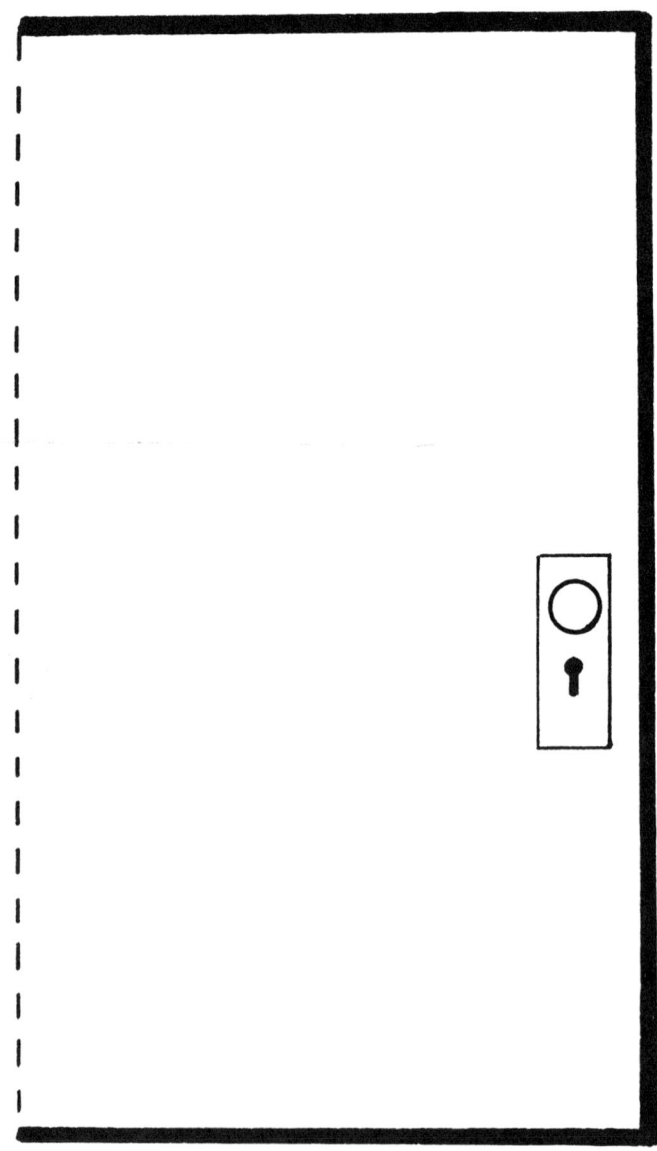

Verbs: Section 1
Activity Sheet 6 (opened)

Name: _____   Date: _____

○   △

is closing    closed

1. **Find the picture that matches.**
   Fill in the blank with the correct word:

○ The raccoon is closing the cage.

△ The raccoon _____ the cage.

close

closed

2. **Write and say:**

closed

_____

_ _ _ _ _ _ _ _ _ _ _ _ _ _ _

_____

33

3. Fill in and say:

Yesterday I _____ the car door.

4. Answer the question. Write your sentence in the blank:

What are some things that you closed this morning?

5. Fill in the missing letters and say the word:

closed

close __

clos __ __

clo __ __ __

cl __ __ __ __

c __ __ __ __ __

Verbs: Section 1
Worksheet 7-2 (closed)

6. Write and say the word four times:

closed

7. Study the two words below.
Then close your eyes and spell:

close

closed

Put a 1 in each little box for your answer.
Add up your answers.
Write the total in this big box.

Verbs: Section 1
Worksheet 7-3 (closed)

Name: _____ **Date:** _____

Cut along the dark line.
Fold the doors open along the dotted line.
Close the doors.

1. **What are you doing?**
2. **What did you do?**
3. **Did you close your own refrigerator door today?**

Verbs: Section 1
Activity Sheet 7 (closed)

Name: _____ **Date:** _____

is climbing

climbed

---

1. **Find the picture that matches.**
   Fill in the blank with the correct word:

   ○ The monkey is climbing the ladder.

   △ The monkey _____ the ladder.

   climbed
   climb

2. **Write and say:**

   climbed

   _____

   – – – – – – – – – – – – – – –

   _____

Verbs: Section 1
Worksheet 8-1 (climbed)

3. Fill in and say:

Yesterday the cat _____ up the tree.

4. Answer the question. Write your sentence in the blank:

What did you climb?

_____
– –
_____
_____
– –
_____

5. Fill in the missing letters and say the word:

climbed

climbe __

climb __ __

clim __ __ __

cli __ __ __ __

cl __ __ __ __ __

c __ __ __ __ __ __

__ __ __ __ __ __ __

score

Verbs: Section 1
Workshop 8-2 (climbed)

6. Write and say the word four times:

climbed

- - - - - - - - - - - - - - - - - -

- - - - - - - - - - - - - - - - - -

- - - - - - - - - - - - - - - - - -

- - - - - - - - - - - - - - - - - -

**7. Study the two words below.
Then close your eyes and spell:**

climb

climbed

Put a 1 in each little box for your answer.
Add up your answers.
Write the total in this big box.

Verbs: Section 1
Worksheet 8-3 (climbed)

Draw a boy climbing the ladder.

1. **What is the boy doing?**
2. **What did he do?**
3. **Did you ever climb a ladder?**
4. **Tell a story about it.**

Name: _____ **Date:** _____

Fill in the blank with the correct word.
Then say the complete sentence:

1. Today the raccoon is closing the cage.

   Yesterday the raccoon _____ the cage.

   close
   closed

2. Yesterday the monkey climbed the ladder.

   Today the monkey _____ the ladder.

   climb
   is climbing

3. Today the pigs are pulling the rope.

   Yesterday the pigs _____ the rope.

   pulled
   pull

4. Yesterday the rabbit opened the door.

   Today the rabbit _____ the door.

   open
   is opening

Verbs: Section 1
Review 2-1

5. Today the monkey is climbing the ladder.

   Yesterday the monkey _____ the ladder.

   climbed
   climb

6. Yesterday the pigs pulled the rope.

   Today the pigs _____ the rope.

   are pulling
   pull

7. Today the rabbit is opening the door.

   Yesterday the rabbit _____ the door.

   opened
   open

8. Yesterday the raccoon closed the cage.

   Today the raccoon _____ the cage.

   close
   is closing

Put a 1 in each little box for your answer.
Add up your answers.
Write the total in this big box.

Name: ______________________ Date: ______________

○

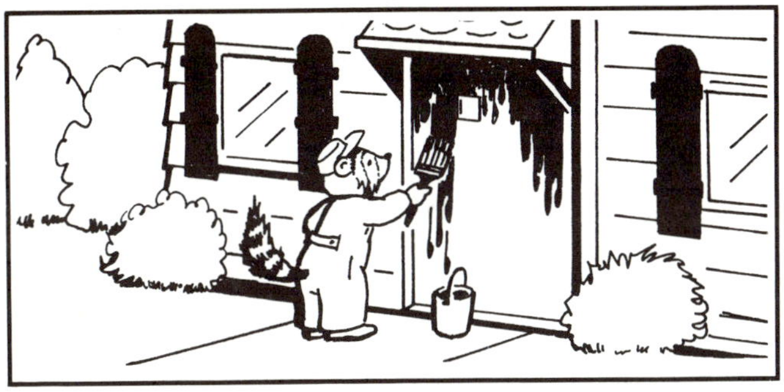

is painting

△

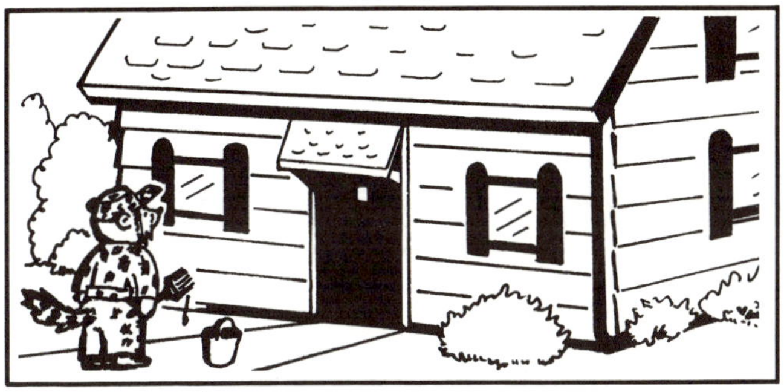

painted

**1. Find the picture that matches.
Fill in the blank with the correct word:**

○ The raccoon is painting the house.

△ The raccoon ______________ the house.

paint

painted

2. Write and say:

painted

Name: _____ Date: _____

3. Fill in and say:

Yesterday the painter _____ the house.

4. Answer the question. Write your sentence in the blank:

What color did the raccoon paint the door?

5. Fill in the missing letters and say the word:

painted

painte __

paint __ __

pain __ __ __

pai __ __ __ __

pa __ __ __ __ __

p __ __ __ __ __ __

__ __ __ __ __ __ __

6. Write and say the word four times:

☐

painted

─────────────────────────────
─ ─ ─ ─ ─ ─ ─ ─ ─ ─ ─ ─ ─ ─ ─
═════════════════════════════
─────────────────────────────
─ ─ ─ ─ ─ ─ ─ ─ ─ ─ ─ ─ ─ ─ ─
═════════════════════════════
─────────────────────────────
─ ─ ─ ─ ─ ─ ─ ─ ─ ─ ─ ─ ─ ─ ─
═════════════════════════════

**7. Study the two words below.
Then close your eyes and spell:**

paint

painted

**Put a 1 in each little box for your answer.
Add up your answers.
Write the total in this big box.**

Verbs: Section 1
Worksheet 9-3 (painted)

Draw a paintbrush in the man's hand.
Help him finish painting the house by coloring it.

1. What are you and the man doing?
2. What color did you and the man paint the house?
3. Tell a story about something you painted.

○   △

is hunting    hunted

1. Find the picture that matches.
   Fill in the blank with the correct word:

○ The bear is hunting for his shoe.

△ The bear _____ for his shoe.

hunted

hunt

2. Write and say:

hunted

_____

_ _ _ _ _ _ _ _ _ _ _ _ _ _

_____

Verbs: Section 1
Worksheet 10-1 (hunted)

Name: _____ Date: _____

3. Fill in and say:

Yesterday we _____ all over the house
for my shoes.

4. Answer the question. Write your sentence in the blank:

Where did you hunt for your missing sock?

_____
- -
_____
_____
- -
_____

5. Fill in the missing letters and say the word:

hunted

hunte __

hunt __ __

hun __ __ __

hu __ __ __ __

h __ __ __ __ __

__ __ __ __ __ __

6. Write and say the word four times:

hunted

- - - - - - - - - - - - - - - -

- - - - - - - - - - - - - - - -

- - - - - - - - - - - - - - - -

- - - - - - - - - - - - - - - -

7. Study the two words below.
Then close your eyes and spell:

hunt

hunted

Put a 1 in each little box for your answer.
Add up your answers.
Write the total in this big box.

Verbs: Section 1
Worksheet 10-3 (hunted)

Name: _____ **Date:** _____

Help the girl hunt for the Easter eggs.
Circle all the eggs and color this page.

1. What is the girl doing?
2. How many eggs did she hunt for?
3. Tell a story about hunting for Easter eggs.

Verbs: Section 1
Activity Sheet 10 (hunted)

○

△

are pointing

pointed

1. Find the picture that matches.
   Fill in the blank with the correct word:

○ The pigs are pointing at the kite.

△ The pigs _____ at the kite.

    point

    pointed

2. Write and say:

    pointed

    _____

    _ _ _ _ _ _ _ _ _ _ _ _ _ _

    _____

Verbs: Section 1
Worksheet 11-1 (pointed)

3. Fill in and say:

Yesterday I _____ at the picture.

4. Answer the question. Write your sentence in the blank:

Did anyone ever point at you? Why?

_____

- -
_____
_____
- -
_____

5. Fill in the missing letters and say the word:

pointed

pointe __

point __ __

poin __ __ __

poi __ __ __ __

po __ __ __ __ __

p __ __ __ __ __ __

__ __ __ __ __ __ __

52
Verbs: Section 1
Worksheet 11-2 (pointed)

6. Write and say the word four times:

pointed

7. Study the two words below.
Then close your eyes and spell:

point

pointed

Put a 1 in each little box for your answer.
Add up your answers.
Write the total in this big box.

Verbs: Section 1
Worksheet 11-3 (pointed)

Name: _____ **Date:** _____

Color the houses.
Point to the open doors.
Point to the closed doors.

What did you do?

Verbs: Section 1
Activity Sheet 11 (pointed)

is adding   added

1. **Find the picture that matches.**
   Fill in the blank with the correct word:

○ The monkey is adding the numbers.

△ The monkey _____ the numbers.

   add

   added

2. **Write and say:**

added

_____

_ _ _ _ _ _ _ _ _ _ _ _ _ _ _

_____

Verbs: Section 1
Worksheet 12-1 (added)

3. Fill in and say:

Yesterday she _____ the numbers wrong.

4. Answer the question. Write your sentence in the blank:

What did you add to your cereal?

_____

– – – – – – – – – – – – – – – – – –

==================================

– – – – – – – – – – – – – – – – – –

==================================

5. Fill in the missing letters and say the word:

added

adde —

add — —

ad — — —

a — — — —

— — — — —

6. Write and say the word four times:

added

⬜

_____

- - - - - - - - - - - - - - - - - - -

_____
_____

- - - - - - - - - - - - - - - - - - -

_____
_____

- - - - - - - - - - - - - - - - - - -

_____
_____

- - - - - - - - - - - - - - - - - - -

7. Study the two words below.
Then close your eyes and spell:

⬜

add

added

Put a 1 in each little box for your answer.
Add up your answers.
Write the total in this big box.

Verbs: Section 1
Worksheet 12-3 (added)

Name: _____ **Date:** _____

Add these numbers.

1. **What are you doing?**
2. **What did you do?**

$$\begin{array}{r} 1 \\ +1 \\ \hline \end{array} \qquad\qquad \begin{array}{r} 3 \\ +2 \\ \hline \end{array}$$

$$\begin{array}{r} 7 \\ +2 \\ \hline \end{array} \qquad\qquad \begin{array}{r} 5 \\ +2 \\ \hline \end{array}$$

$$\begin{array}{r} 8 \\ +1 \\ \hline \end{array} \qquad\qquad \begin{array}{r} 6 \\ +3 \\ \hline \end{array}$$

$$\begin{array}{r} 4 \\ +3 \\ \hline \end{array} \qquad\qquad \begin{array}{r} 2 \\ +4 \\ \hline \end{array}$$

Verbs: Section 1
Activity Sheet 12 (added)

Fill in the blank with the correct word.
Then say the complete sentence:

1. Yesterday the pigs pointed at the kite.

   Today the pigs _____ at the kite.

   are pointing
   point   ☐

2. Today the monkey is adding numbers.

   Yesterday the monkey _____ numbers.

   add
   added   ☐

3. Yesterday the raccoon painted the house.

   Today the raccoon _____ the house.

   paint
   is painting   ☐

4. Today the bear is hunting for his shoes.

   Yesterday the bear _____ for his shoes.

   hunt
   hunted   ☐

5. Yesterday the monkey added numbers.

Today the monkey _____ numbers.

add
is adding

6. Today the raccoon is painting the house.

Yesterday the raccoon _____ the house.

painted
paint

7. Yesterday the bear hunted for his shoes.

Today the bear _____ for his shoes.

is hunting
hunt

8. Today the pigs are pointing at the rope.

Yesterday the pigs _____ at the rope.

point
pointed

Put a 1 in each little box for your answer.
Add up your answers.
Write the total in this big box.

Verbs: Section 1
Review 3-2

Picture Summary

Teacher:
On the following page is a picture summary. Look at the picture with the student and discuss what all of the animals are doing. First use the present progressive tense.

is walking
is pushing
is hopping
is talking
is pulling
is opening
is closing
is climbing
is painting
is hunting
is pointing
is adding

Then say, "This picture was taken yesterday. Tell me what each animal did." Encourage the student to use each of the 12 verbs covered in the section in the past tense.

63

Verbs: Section 1
Picture Summary 1-2

Mix & Match Game

Teacher:
Make flashcards of pictures 1a/b through 12a/b.
Laminate the pictures for prolonged use.

1. Shuffle flashcards and place face down on the table.
2. Choose player to begin game.
3. Player turns over one card and says the word.
4. Then player turns over another card.
5. If it matches the first card (for example, open, opened), player makes up a sentence using the past tense verb.
6. After a match is made, the player takes another turn.
7. If cards do not match, they are turned face down and it is the next player's turn.
8. Player with the greatest number of pairs is the winner.

Name: _____ **Date:** _____

Writing Sentences

Write a sentence for each of these words:

1. closed _____ ☐

2. hunted _____ ☐

3. opened _____ ☐

4. hopped _____ ☐

5. pulled _____ ☐

6. pointed _____ ☐

Verbs: Section 1
Summary 1-1

7. climbed _____ ☐

8. added _____ ☐

9. walked _____ ☐

10. painted _____ ☐

Put a 1 in each little box for your answer.
Add up your answers.
Write the total in this big box.

Verbs: Section 1
Summary 1-2

Name: _____ Date: _____

Fill in the blank with the correct word:

The Tree House

It was Saturday morning. Steve _____ out
        (hop, hopped)

of bed. He _____ on his pants, and picked up a
        (pull, pulled)

paint can. After he _____ for a paintbrush,
        (hunt, hunted)

he was ready to go. Steve went outside, and _____
                (close, closed)

the door. He _____ down the path to the
        (walk, walked)

woods. When he got to the tree house, there was Sally.

She _____ up the ladder and went into the
    (climb, climbed)

tree house. Steve _____ at her. He was very
            (point, pointed)

mad. But after he _____ to Sally, Steve
            (talk, talked)

decided she could stay. After they _____ the
                    (paint, painted)

tree house, it was time to go home. They _____
                        (climb, climbed)

down the ladder. Steve said "Goodbye." Then he

_____, "You can come back again, Sally."
    (add, added)

Steve had more fun that day because he shared his tree

house with a friend.

_____

Count the number of answers.
Write that number in this box.

_____

Name: _____

Progress Chart 1

Worksheet Number	Verbs	Date	Questions Completed	Total Possible
1.	walked			7
2.	pushed			7
3.	hopped			7
4.	talked			7
Review 1				10
5.	pulled			7
6.	opened			7
7.	closed			7
8.	climbed			7
Review 2				10
9.	painted			7
10.	hunted			7
11.	pointed			7
12.	added			7
Review 3				10
Summary 1				10
Summary 2				14

Shape Up Your Language

Part I: Verbs — Past Tense

Section 2

Pre/Post-Test Sheet 2 72
found (13a/b)   Worksheet 13 73
                 Activity Sheet 13 76
ate (14a/b)   Worksheet 14 77
                 Activity Sheet 14 80
sat (15a/b)   Worksheet 15 81
                 Activity Sheet 15 84
took (16a/b)   Worksheet 16 85
                 Activity Sheet 16 88
Review 4 89

broke (17a/b)   Worksheet 17 91
                 Activity Sheet 17 94
drank (18a/b)   Worksheet 18 95
                 Activity Sheet 18 98
shook (19a/b)   Worksheet 19 99
                 Activity Sheet 19 102
wore (20a/b)   Worksheet 20 103
                 Activity Sheet 20 106
Review 5 108

slept (21a/b)   Worksheet 21 111
                 Activity Sheet 21 114
fed (22a/b)   Worksheet 22 115
                 Activity Sheet 22 118
swept (23a/b)   Worksheet 23 119
                 Activity Sheet 23 122
brought (24a/b)   Worksheet 24 123
                 Activity Sheet 24 127
Review 6 128

Picture Summary 2 130
Game 2: Snail Game 132
Summary Worksheet 3: Writing Sentences 134
Summary Worksheet 4: Circle the Word 136
Progress Chart 2 137

Name: _____

Pre/Post-Test Sheet (Verbs: Section 2)

Make flashcards of pictures 13a/b through 24a/b. See page 1 of manual.

Pre-Test	Date: _____	correct	incorrect	Post-Test	Date: _____	correct	incorrect
13	found			13	found		
14	ate			14	ate		
15	sat			15	sat		
16	took			16	took		
17	broke			17	broke		
18	drank			18	drank		
19	shook			19	shook		
20	wore			20	wore		
21	slept			21	slept		
22	fed			22	fed		
23	swept			23	swept		
24	brought			24	brought		

Post-Test Objective: The student will achieve 85% accuracy (10 out of 12 words). Repeat entire section if objective is not met.

Verbs: Section 2
Pre/Post-Test Sheet 2

Name: _____ **Date:** _____

○

△

is finding   found

1. Find the picture that matches.
Fill in the blank with the correct word:

○ The bear is finding the eggs.

△ The bear _____ the eggs.

find
found

2. Write and say:

is finding   found

_____   _____

- - - - - - - - - -   - - - - - - - - - -

_____   _____

Verbs: Section 2
Worksheet 13-1 (found)

3. **Fill in and say:**

Yesterday I _____ a penny.

4. **Answer the question. Write your sentence in the blank:**

Where did you find your shoes this morning?

_____

- -

_____

- -

_____

5. **Fill in the missing letters and say the word:**

find   found

fin __   foun __

fi __ __   fou __ __

f __ __ __   fo __ __ __

__ __ __ __   f __ __ __ __

               __ __ __ __ __

Verbs: Section 2
Worksheet 13-2 (found)

6. Write and say the word four times:

find   found

- - - - - - - - - - - -   - - - - - - - - - - - -

- - - - - - - - - - - -   - - - - - - - - - - - -

- - - - - - - - - - - -   - - - - - - - - - - - -
---

7. Study the two words below.
Then close your eyes and spell:

find

found

Put a 1 in each little box for your answer.
Add up your answers.
Write the total in this big box.

Name: _____ Date: _____

Find something to write with. Circle it.
Find something to comb your hair with. Circle it.
Find something to look into. Circle it.

1. What did you find to write with?

2. What did you find to comb your hair with?

3. What did you find to look into?

Name: _____ **Date:** _____

is eating   ate

1. Find the picture that matches.
   Fill in the blank with the correct word:

○ The raccoon is eating the banana.

△ The raccoon _____ the banana.

ate

eat

2. Write and say:

is eating   ate

_____   _____

- - - - - - - - - - - - -   - - - - - - - - - - - - -

_____   _____

Verbs: Section 2
Worksheet 14-1 (ate)

3. Fill in and say:

Yesterday I _____ a hamburger.

4. Answer the question. Write your sentence in the blank:

What did you eat for breakfast?

5. Fill in the missing letters and say the word:

eat   ate

ea __   at __

e __ __   a __ __

__ __ __   __ __ __

6. Write and say the word four times:

eat   ate

_____   _____
– – – – – – – – – – – –   – – – – – – – – – – – –
_____   _____
_____   _____
– – – – – – – – – – – –   – – – – – – – – – – – –
_____   _____
_____   _____
– – – – – – – – – – – –   – – – – – – – – – – – –
_____   _____
_____   _____
– – – – – – – – – – – –   – – – – – – – – – – – –

**7. Study the two words below.
Then close your eyes and spell:**

eat

ate

Put a 1 in each little box for your answer.
Add up your answers.
Write the total in this big box.

Verbs: Section 2
Worksheet 14-3 (ate)

Color and cut out the foods.
Place each food on or beside the plate.

1. What did you eat for breakfast this morning?
2. What did you eat for breakfast yesterday morning?

Verbs: Section 2
Activity Sheet 14 (ate)

○

△

is sitting

sat

1. Find the picture that matches.
Fill in the blank with the correct word:

○ The bear is sitting down.

△ The bear _____ down.

sat

sit

2. Write and say:

is sitting

sat

_____

- - - - - - - - - - -

_____

_____

- - - - - - - - - - - -

_____

Verbs: Section 2
Worksheet 15-1 (sat)

3. Fill in and say:

Yesterday he _____ in the big chair.

4. Answer the question. Write your sentence in the blank:

Where are some places you sat this morning?

_____
- - - - - - - - - - - - - - - - - - - -
_____
_____
- - - - - - - - - - - - - - - - - - - -
_____

5. Fill in the missing letters and say the word:

sit   sat

si ___   sa ___

s ___ ___   s ___ ___

___ ___ ___   ___ ___ ___

Verbs: Section 2
Worksheet 15-2 (sat)

6. Write and say the word four times:

sit

sat

7. Study the two words below.
Then close your eyes and spell:

sit

sat

Put a 1 in each little box for your answer.
Add up your answers.
Write the total in this big box.

Verbs: Section 2
Worksheet 15-3 (sat)

Do you know the story of Goldilocks and the Three Bears?
Answer the questions. Write your answers in the blanks.
1. Which chair did the baby bear sit in?
   He _____
2. Which chair did the mama bear sit in?
   She _____
3. Which chair did the papa bear sit in?
   He _____

Color and cut out the bears and chairs.
Put the bears in their own chairs.

Verbs: Section 2
Activity Sheet 15 (sat)

○

△

is taking

took

1. **Find the picture that matches.**
   Fill in the blank with the correct word:

○ The monkey is taking the bananas.

△ The monkey _____ the bananas.

took

take

2. **Write and say:**

is taking

took

_____   _____

_ _ _ _ _ _ _ _ _ _ _   _ _ _ _ _ _ _ _ _ _ _

3. Fill in and say:

I _____ my dog for a walk yesterday.

4. Answer the question. Write your sentence in the blank:

What did you take home yesterday?

5. Fill in the missing letters and say the word:

take   took

tak __   too __

ta __ __   to __ __

t __ __ __   t __ __ __

__ __ __ __   __ __ __ __

6. Write and say the word four times:

take   took

took

take

Put a 1 in each little box for your answer.
Add up your answers.
Write the total in this big box.

Verbs: Section 2
Worksheet 16-3 (took)

Name: _____ **Date:** _____

Color and cut out the picture cards.

Let's play Missing-Pictures.
1. Choose a partner.
2. Close your eyes while your partner takes a picture and hides it under the table or under a book.
3. Your partner will ask, "Which picture did I take?"
4. You will answer, "You took the _____."
5. If your answer is correct, it's your turn to take a picture.

Verbs: Section 2
Activity Sheet 16 (took)

Name: _____ **Date:** _____

Fill in the blank with the correct word.
Then say the complete sentence:

1. Yesterday the bear walked to the store.

    Now the bear _____ to the store.

    walk

    is walking   □

2. Today the bear is sitting on the mushroom.

    Yesterday the bear _____ on the mushroom.

    sit

    sat   □

3. Yesterday the raccoon ate a banana.

    Now the raccoon _____ a banana.

    eat

    is eating   □

4. Now the monkey is taking bananas.

    Yesterday the monkey _____ bananas.

    take

    took   □

5. Yesterday the bear found his shoe.

    Now the bear _____ his shoe.

    find

    is finding   □

Verbs: Section 2
Review 4-1

6. Today the bear is walking to the store.

   Yesterday the bear _____ to the store.

   walk

   walked

7. Yesterday the bear sat on the mushroom.

   Today the bear _____ on the mushroom.

   sit

   is sitting

8. Now the raccoon is eating a banana.

   Yesterday the raccoon _____ a banana.

   eat

   ate

9. Yesterday the monkey took bananas.

   Now the monkey _____ bananas.

   take

   is taking

10. Now the bear is finding his shoe.

    Yesterday the bear _____ his shoe.

    find

    found

Put a 1 in each little box for your answer.
Add up your answers.
Write the total in this big box.

Verbs: Section 2
Review 4-2

Name: _____ Date: _____

○ △

are breaking   broke

1. **Find the picture that matches.**
   Fill in the blank with the correct word:

○ The bears are breaking the wishbone.

△ The bears _____ the wishbone.

break
broke

2. **Write and say:**

are breaking   broke

_____   _____

_ _ _ _ _ _ _ _ _ _ _ _ _   _ _ _ _ _ _ _ _ _ _ _ _ _

_____   _____

Verbs: Section 2
Worksheet 17-1 (broke)

3. Fill in and say:

Yesterday I _____ a wishbone.

4. Answer the question. Write your sentence in the blank:

The last time you knocked a glass off the table, what happened?

_____

— — — — — — — — — — — — — — — — — —

_____

_____

— — — — — — — — — — — — — — — — — —

_____

5. Fill in the missing letters and say the word:

break   broke

brea __   brok __

bre __ __   bro __ __

br __ __ __   br __ __ __

b __ __ __ __   b __ __ __ __

— — — — —   — — — — —

Verbs: Section 2
Worksheet 17-2 (broke)

6. Write and say the word four times:

break   broke

_____   _____
- - - - - - - - - - - - - -   - - - - - - - - - - - - - -
_____   _____
_____   _____
- - - - - - - - - - - - - -   - - - - - - - - - - - - - -
_____   _____
_____   _____
- - - - - - - - - - - - - -   - - - - - - - - - - - - - -
_____   _____
_____   _____
- - - - - - - - - - - - - -   - - - - - - - - - - - - - -
_____   _____

**7. Study the two words below.
Then close your eyes and spell:**

break

broke

**Put a 1 in each little box for your answer.
Add up your answers.
Write the total in this big box.**

Verbs: Section 2
Worksheet 17-3 (broke)

Name: _____ **Date:** _____

Draw a picture of some things breaking.

1. **Tell what is happening.**
2. **Tell what happened.**

Verbs: Section 2
Activity Sheet 17 (broke)

○   △

is drinking   drank

1. Find the picture that matches.
   Fill in the blank with the correct word:

○ The pig is drinking the water.

△ The pig _____ the water.

drank

drink

2. Write and say:

is drinking   drank

_____   _____

– – – – – – – – –   – – – – – – – – –

_____   _____

Verbs: Section 2
Worksheet 18-1 (drank)

3. Fill in and say:

Yesterday I _____ all of my milk.

4. Answer the question. Write your sentence in the blank:

What did you drink at lunch yesterday?

_____

- -
_____
_____
- -
_____

5. Fill in the missing letters and say the word:

drink	drank
drin _	dran _
dri _ _	dra _ _
dr _ _ _	dr _ _ _
d _ _ _ _	d _ _ _ _
_ _ _ _ _	_ _ _ _ _

Verbs: Section 2
Worksheet 18-2 (drank)

6. Write and say the word four times:

drink   drank

7. Study the two words below.
Then close your eyes and spell:

drink

drank

Put a 1 in each little box for your answer.
Add up your answers.
Write the total in this big box.

Verbs: Section 2
Worksheet 18-3 (drank)

Name: _____ **Date:** _____

Color each drink.
Write the name of each drink under the picture.

1. Pretend you are eating breakfast. What are you drinking?
2. What did you drink this morning?
3. Pretend you are eating dinner. What are you drinking?
4. What did you drink last night?
5. Pretend you are eating lunch. What are you drinking?
6. Pretend you are at a picnic. What are you drinking?

_____   _____   _____

_____   _____   _____

Verbs: Section 2
Activity Sheet 18 (drank)

is shaking   shook

**1. Find the picture that matches.
Find the blank with the correct word:**

○ The monkey is shaking the tree.

△ The monkey _____ the tree.

shook

shake

2. Write and say:

is shaking   shook

_____   _____

— — — — — — — — — —   — — — — — — — — — —

Verbs: Section 2
Worksheet 19-1 (shook)

3. **Fill in and say:**

Yesterday I _____ all of the rugs.

4. **Answer the question. Write your sentence in the blank:**

Did you ever shake a bottle of pop before opening it?

What happened?

_____

- -

_____
_____

- -

_____

5. **Fill in the missing letters and say the word:**

shake	shook
shak __	shoo __
sha __ __	sho __ __
sh __ __ __	sh __ __ __
s __ __ __ __	s __ __ __ __
__ __ __ __ __	__ __ __ __ __

Verbs: Section 2
Worksheet 19-2 (shook)

6. Write and say the word four times:

shake   shook

‾‾‾‾‾‾‾‾‾‾‾‾‾‾‾‾‾‾‾‾‾‾‾‾‾‾   ‾‾‾‾‾‾‾‾‾‾‾‾‾‾‾‾‾‾‾‾‾‾‾‾‾‾

- - - - - - - - - - - - -   - - - - - - - - - - - - -

‾‾‾‾‾‾‾‾‾‾‾‾‾‾‾‾‾‾‾‾‾‾‾‾‾‾   ‾‾‾‾‾‾‾‾‾‾‾‾‾‾‾‾‾‾‾‾‾‾‾‾‾‾

- - - - - - - - - - - - -   - - - - - - - - - - - - -

‾‾‾‾‾‾‾‾‾‾‾‾‾‾‾‾‾‾‾‾‾‾‾‾‾‾   ‾‾‾‾‾‾‾‾‾‾‾‾‾‾‾‾‾‾‾‾‾‾‾‾‾‾

- - - - - - - - - - - - -   - - - - - - - - - - - - -

‾‾‾‾‾‾‾‾‾‾‾‾‾‾‾‾‾‾‾‾‾‾‾‾‾‾   ‾‾‾‾‾‾‾‾‾‾‾‾‾‾‾‾‾‾‾‾‾‾‾‾‾‾

7. Study the two words below.
Then close your eyes and spell:

shake

shook

Put a 1 in each little box for your answer.
Add up your answers.
Write the total in this big box.

Verbs: Section 2
Worksheet 19-3 (shook)

Name: _____ **Date:** _____

Find pictures of things you shake. Circle them.

1. Pretend you are shaking the things you circled.
   Tell about it.
2. What did you shake?

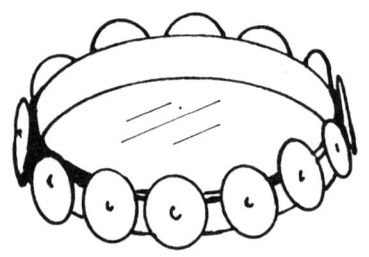

tambourine

telephone

glasses

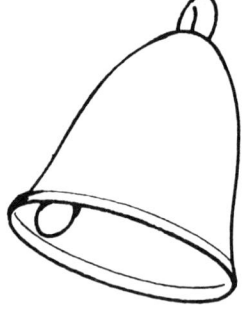

bell

rattle

salt and pepper shakers

Verbs: Section 2
Activity Sheet 19 (shook)

Name: _____ **Date:** _____

○

△

is wearing   wore

1. **Find the picture that matches.**
   Fill in the blank with the correct word:

○ The monkey is wearing the hat.

△ The monkey _____ the hat.

   wore

   wear

2. **Write and say:**

   is wearing   wore

   _____   _____
   - - - - - - - - - - -   - - - - - - - - - - -
   _____   _____

Verbs: Section 2
Worksheet 20-1 (wore)

3. Fill in and say:

Yesterday she _____ her new shoes.

4. Answer the question. Write your sentence in the blank:

What did you wear to school yesterday?

‾‾

- - - - - - - - - - - - - - - - - - - -

‾‾

- - - - - - - - - - - - - - - - - - - -

‾‾

5. Fill in the missing letters and say the word:

wear	wore
wea __	wor __
we __ __	wo __ __
w __ __ __	w __ __ __
__ __ __ __	__ __ __ __

Verbs: Section 2
Worksheet 20-2 (wore)

6. Write and say the word four times:

wear   wore

_____   _____

- - - - - - - - - - - - - -   - - - - - - - - - - - - - -
_____   _____

- - - - - - - - - - - - - -   - - - - - - - - - - - - - -
_____   _____

- - - - - - - - - - - - - -   - - - - - - - - - - - - - -
_____   _____

- - - - - - - - - - - - - -   - - - - - - - - - - - - - -
_____   _____

7. Study the two words below.
Then close your eyes and spell:

wear

wore

Put a 1 in each little box for your answer.
Add up your answers.
Write the total in this big box.

Verbs: Section 2
Worksheet 20-3 (wore)

Name: _____ Date: _____

Color the girl and the boy. Color the shirt blue.
Color the pants brown. Color the skirt red. Color the blouse green.
Cut out the girl, the boy, and the clothes.
Dress the girl and the boy.

1. What is the girl wearing?
2. What is the boy wearing?
3. What did they wear before you dressed them?

Name: _____ Date: _____

Verbs: Section 2
Activity Sheet 20-2 (wore)

Fill in the blank with the correct word.
Then say the complete sentence:

1. Yesterday the monkey shook the tree.

   Today the monkey _____ the tree.

   shake

   is shaking

2. Now the bears are breaking the wishbone.

   Yesterday the bears _____ the wishbone.

   break

   broke

3. Yesterday the kangaroo hopped.

   Today the kangaroo _____.

   hop

   is hopping

4. Now the pig is drinking.

   Yesterday the pig _____.

   drank

   drink

5. Yesterday the monkey wore a hat.

   Today the monkey _____ a hat.

   is wearing

   wore

Verbs: Section 2
Review 5-1

6. Now the monkey is shaking the tree.

Yesterday the monkey _____ the tree.

shake

shook

☐

7. Yesterday the bears broke the wishbone.

Now the bears _____ the wishbone.

break

are breaking

☐

8. Today the kangaroo is hopping.

Yesterday the kangaroo _____.

hopped

hop

☐

9. Yesterday the pig drank.

Now the pig _____.

drink

is drinking

☐

10. Today the monkey is wearing a hat.

Yesterday the monkey _____ a hat.

wore

wear

☐

Put a 1 in each little box for your answer.
Add up your answers.
Write the total in this big box.

Name: _____ **Date:** _____

⃝

△

is sleeping

slept

1. **Find the picture that matches.**
   Fill in the blank with the correct word:

⃝ The bear is sleeping.

△ The bear _____.

   sleep

   slept

2. **Write and say:**

   is sleeping

   slept

   _ _ _ _ _ _ _ _ _ _   _ _ _ _ _ _ _ _ _ _

Verbs: Section 2
Worksheet 21-1 (slept)

3. Fill in and say:

Snow White _____ for 100 years.

4. Answer the question. Write your sentence in the blank:

Think about an animal you know.

Where did it sleep last night?

_____

- -

_____

- -

_____

5. Fill in the missing letters and say the word:

sleep	slept
slee __	slep __
sle __ __	sle __ __
sl __ __ __	sl __ __ __
s __ __ __ __	s __ __ __ __
__ __ __ __ __	__ __ __ __ __

Verbs: Section 2
Worksheet 21-2 (slept)

6. Write and say the word four times:

sleep   slept

⬜

_____   _____

- - - - - - - - - - - - - -   - - - - - - - - - - - - - -
_____   _____

- - - - - - - - - - - - - -   - - - - - - - - - - - - - -
_____   _____

- - - - - - - - - - - - - -   - - - - - - - - - - - - - -
_____   _____

- - - - - - - - - - - - - -   - - - - - - - - - - - - - -
_____   _____

7. Study the two words below.
   Then close your eyes and spell:

⬜

sleep

slept

Put a 1 in each little box for your answer.
Add up your answers.
Write the total in this big box.

Verbs: Section 2
Worksheet 21-3 (slept)

Name: _____ **Date:** _____

Ask your friends how long they slept last night.
Write it down on the chart below.
Report the results like this:
    "Last night Bob slept for nine hours."

How long did you sleep last night?

Name	Hours
_____	_____
_____	_____
_____	_____
_____	_____
_____	_____
_____	_____
_____	_____
_____	_____

Verbs: Section 2
Activity Sheet 21 (slept)

Name: _____ **Date:** _____

◯

△

is feeding

fed

1. Find the picture that matches.
Fill in the blank with the correct word:

◯ The mother is feeding the baby.

△ The mother _____ the baby.

feed

fed

2. Write and say:

is feeding

fed

_____

_ _ _ _ _ _ _ _ _ _

_____

_ _ _ _ _ _ _ _ _ _

Verbs: Section 2
Worksheet 22-1 (fed)

Name: _____ **Date:** _____

3. Fill in and say:

Yesterday I _____ my baby sister.

4. Answer the question. Write your sentence in the blank:

What animals did you feed last year?

_____

- -
═══════════════════════════════════════
- -
_____

5. Fill in the missing letters and say the word:

feed   fed

fee __   fe __

fe __ __   f __ __

f __ __ __   __ __ __

__ __ __ __

6. Write and say the word four times:

feed

fed

_____   _____
– – – – – – – – – – – – – – – –   – – – – – – – – – – – – – – – –
_____   _____
– – – – – – – – – – – – – – – –   – – – – – – – – – – – – – – – –
_____   _____
– – – – – – – – – – – – – – – –   – – – – – – – – – – – – – – – –
_____   _____

7. Study the two words below.
   Then close your eyes and spell:

feed

fed

Put a 1 in each little box for your answer.
Add up your answers.
Write the total in this big box.

Verbs: Section 2
Worksheet 22-3 (fed)

Name: _____ **Date:** _____

Some zoos let you feed some of the animals.
Draw a picture of someone feeding an animal.

1. What is the person feeding the animal?
2. What did you feed an animal?

Verbs: Section 2
Activity Sheet 22 (fed)

○   △

is sweeping   swept

1. Find the picture that matches.
   Fill in the blank with the correct word:

○ The rabbit is sweeping the floor.

△ The rabbit _____ the floor.

swept

sweep

2. Write and say:

is sweeping   swept

_____   _____

\- \- \- \- \- \- \- \- \-   \- \- \- \- \- \- \- \- \-

_____   _____

Verbs: Section 2
Worksheet 23-1 (swept)

3. Fill in and say:

Cinderella _____ the floor, then she
went to the ball.

4. Answer the question. Write your sentence in the blank:

When was the last time you swept the floor?

_____

5. Fill in the missing letters and say the word:

sweep	swept
swee __	swep __
swe __ __	swe __ __
sw __ __ __	sw __ __ __
s __ __ __ __	s __ __ __ __
__ __ __ __ __	__ __ __ __ __

6. Write and say the word four times:

sweep   swept

‾‾‾‾‾‾‾‾‾‾‾‾‾‾‾‾‾‾‾‾‾‾‾‾‾‾‾‾‾‾‾‾

7. Study the two words below.
Then close your eyes and spell:

sweep

swept

Put a 1 in each little box for your answer.
Add up your answers.
Write the total in this big box.

Verbs: Section 2
Worksheet 23-3 (swept)

Name: _____ **Date:** _____

Color the brooms.

1. Do you sweep with a broom like Broom A or like Broom B?
2. What do you sweep?
3. When was the last time you swept something?
4. What did you sweep?

Broom A   Broom B

Verbs: Section 2
Activity Sheet 23 (swept)

○

△

is bringing

brought

1. Find the picture that matches.
   Fill in the blank with the correct word:

○ The raccoon is bringing flowers.

△ The raccoon _____ flowers.

bring

brought

2. Write and say:

is bringing   brought

_____   _____

- - - - - - - - - - - - -   - - - - - - - - - - - - -

_____   _____

123

Verbs: Section 2
Worksheet 24-1 (brought)

3. Fill in and say:

We _____ hot dogs to the picnic yesterday.

4. Answer the question. Write your sentence in the blank:

What did you bring to school today?

_____

- -

_____
_____

- -

_____

5. Fill in the missing letters and say the word:

bring   brought

brin __   brough __

bri __ __   broug __ __

br __ __ __   brou __ __ __

b __ __ __ __   bro __ __ __ __

__ __ __ __ __   br __ __ __ __ __

                         b __ __ __ __ __ __

                         __ __ __ __ __ __ __

Verbs: Section 2
Worksheet 24-2 (brought)

6. Write and say the word four times:

bring   brought

_____   _____
- - - - - - - - -   - - - - - - - - -
_____   _____
- - - - - - - - -   - - - - - - - - -
_____   _____
- - - - - - - - -   - - - - - - - - -
_____   _____
- - - - - - - - -   - - - - - - - - -

7. Study the two words below.
   Then close your eyes and spell:

bring

brought

Put a 1 in each little box for your answer.
Add up your answers.
Write the total in this big box.

Verbs: Section 2
Worksheet 24-3 (brought)

Name: _____ **Date:** _____

Color the suitcase.
Color and cut out the shell, book, toy, and candy bar.
Paste them in the suitcase.

Pretend that you went on a trip.
What did you bring home with you?

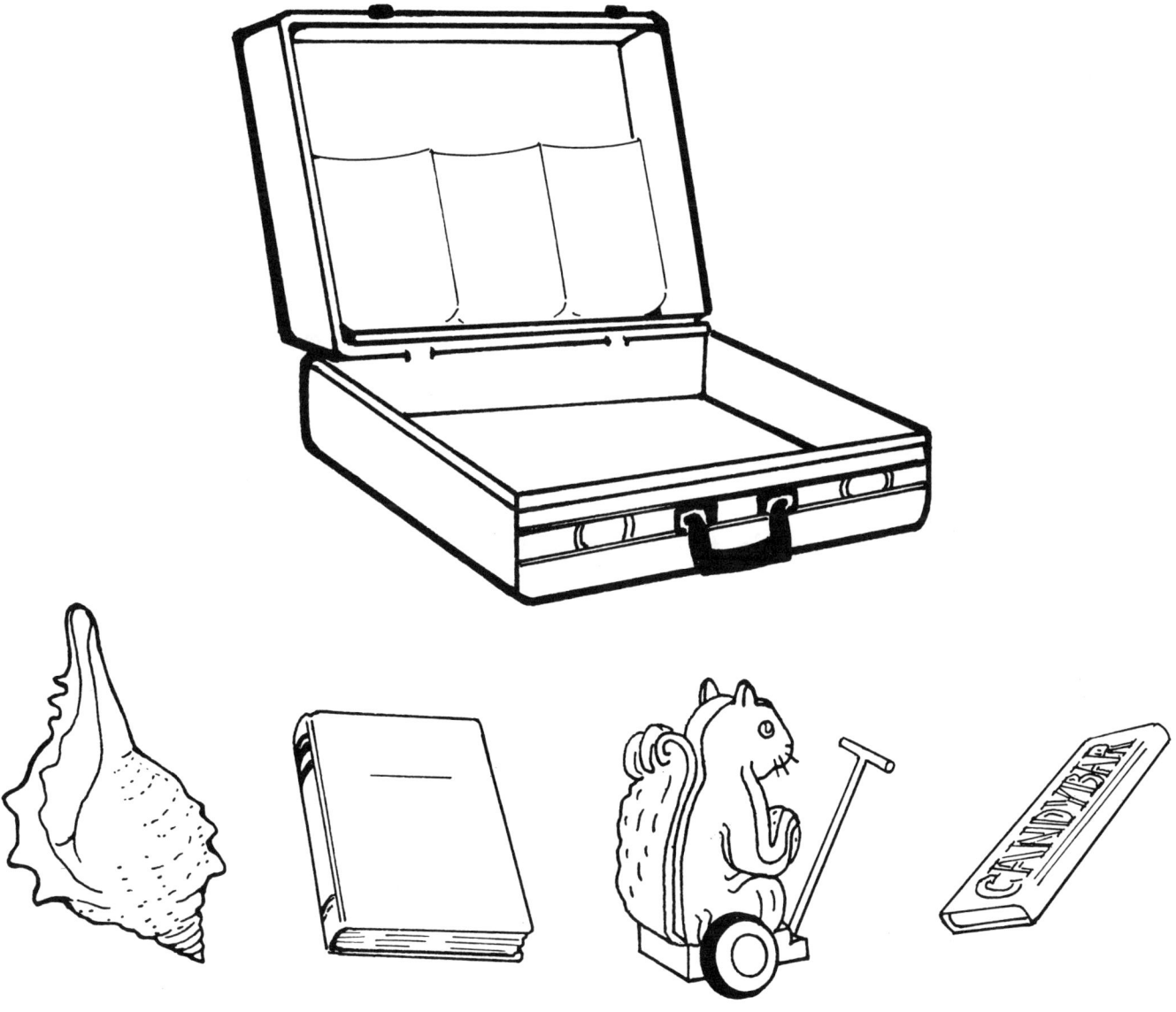

Verbs: Section 2
Activity Sheet 24 (brought)

Name: _____ **Date:** _____

Fill in the blank with the correct word.
Then say the complete sentence:

1. Yesterday the bear slept.

   Today the bear _____.

   sleep

   is sleeping

2. Now the rabbit is sweeping.

   Yesterday the rabbit _____.

   swept

   sweep

3. Yesterday the raccoon brought flowers.

   Today the raccoon _____ flowers.

   bring

   is bringing

4. Now the kangaroo is feeding her baby.

   Yesterday the kangaroo _____ her baby.

   feed

   fed

5. Yesterday the rabbit talked on the phone.

   Now the rabbit _____ on the phone.

   is talking

   talk

Verbs: Section 2
Review 6-1

6. Today the bear is sleeping.

   Yesterday the bear _____.

   slept

   is sleeping

   ☐

7. Yesterday the rabbit swept the floor.

   Now the rabbit _____ the floor.

   is sweeping

   sweep

   ☐

8. Today the raccoon is bringing flowers.

   Yesterday the raccoon _____ flowers.

   brought

   bring

   ☐

9. Yesterday the kangaroo fed her baby.

   Now the kangaroo _____ her baby.

   feed

   is feeding

   ☐

10. Now the rabbit is talking on the phone.

    Yesterday the rabbit _____ on the phone.

    talk

    talked

    ☐

Put a 1 in each little box for your answer.
Add up your answers.
Write the total in this big box.

Verbs: Section 2
Review 6-2

Picture Summary

Teacher:

On the following page is a picture summary. Look at the picture with the student and discuss what all of the animals are doing. First use the present progressive tense.

is finding

is eating

is sitting

is taking

is breaking

is drinking

is shaking

is wearing

is sleeping

is feeding

is sweeping

is bringing

Then say, "This picture was taken yesterday. Tell me what each animal did." Encourage the student to use each of the 12 verbs covered in the section in the past tense.

Name: _____ Date: _____

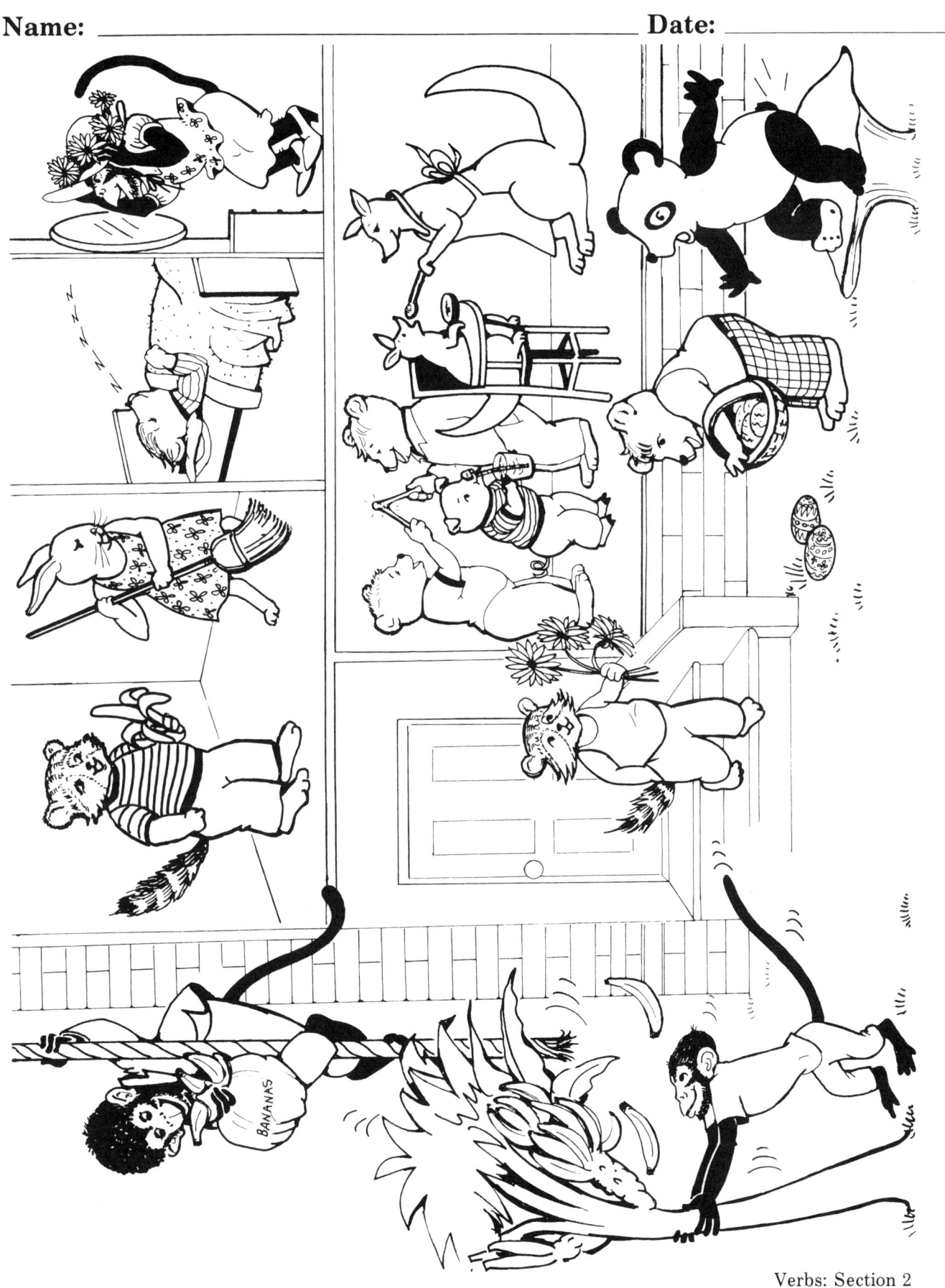

Verbs: Section 2
Picture Summary 2-2

Snail Game

Teacher:

1. Give each player a marker.
2. Have all the markers placed on START.
3. For each turn, a player rolls a die and moves the marker counter-clockwise for the number of spaces indicated on the die.
4. When landing on a space, the player reads the word on that space and gives the past tense. If the word has a star next to it, the player must use that word in a sentence.
5. If an incorrect response is given, the player rolls the die again and moves backward the number of spaces shown on the die.
6. The player who reaches END first wins the game.

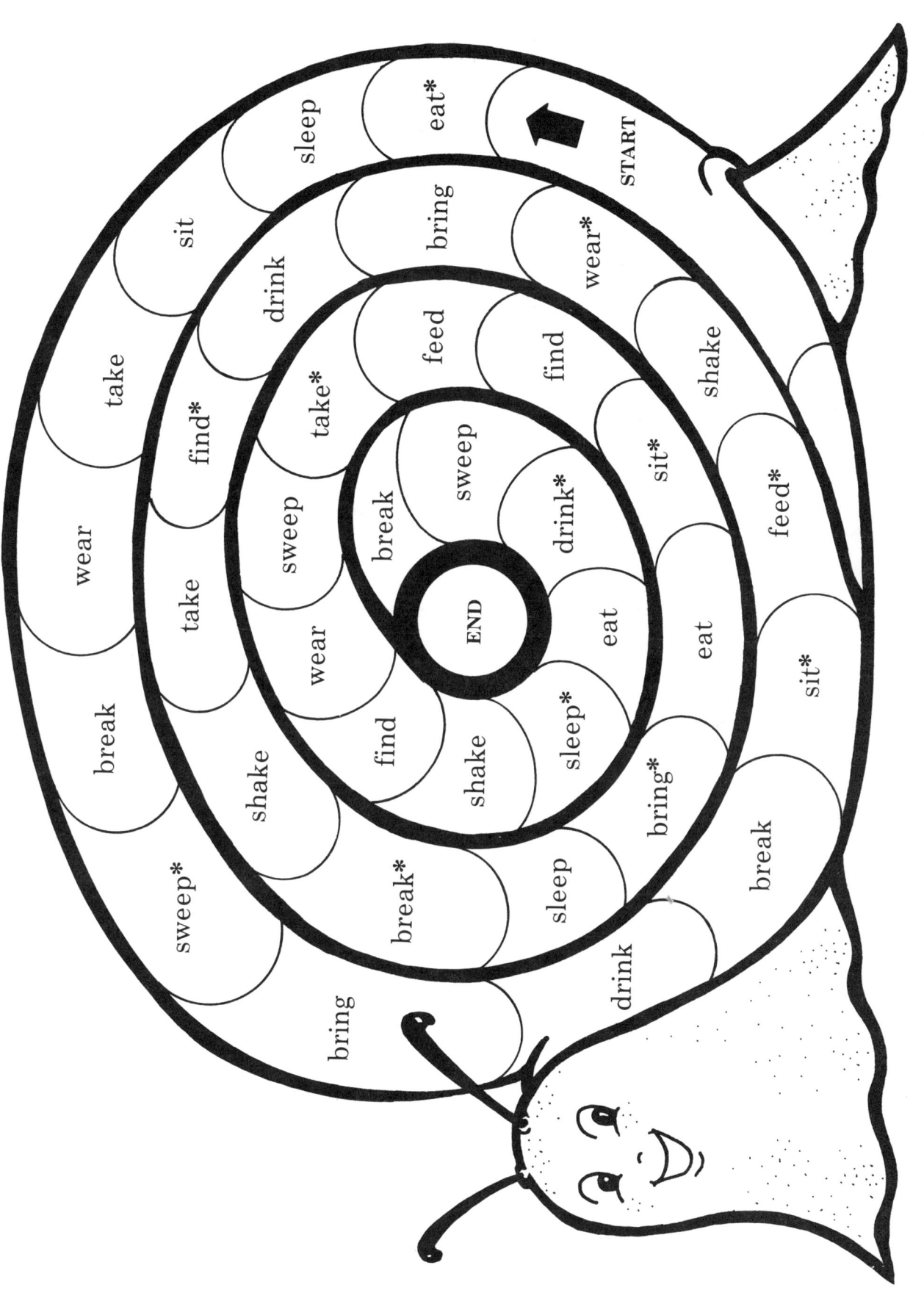

START

eat*

sleep

sit

drink

bring

take

find*

wear*

feed

take*

find

shake

wear

sweep

break

feed*

break

sweep

sit*

shake

eat

sit*

find

break*

shake

sweep*

END

drink*

eat

bring*

break

bring

sleep*

sleep

drink

Verbs: Section 2
Game 2-2

Name: _____ **Date:** _____

Writing Sentences

Write a sentence for each of these words:

1. found

   ─────────────────────────────────── □

2. slept

   ─────────────────────────────────── □

3. broke

   ─────────────────────────────────── □

4. ate

   ─────────────────────────────────── □

5. shook

   ─────────────────────────────────── □

6. drank

   ─────────────────────────────────── □

Verbs: Section 2
Summary 3-1

7. sat

_____ [ ]
- - - - - - - - - - - - - - - - - - -
_____

8. wore

_____ [ ]
- - - - - - - - - - - - - - - - - - -
_____

9. took

_____ [ ]
- - - - - - - - - - - - - - - - - - -
_____

10. swept

_____ [ ]
- - - - - - - - - - - - - - - - - - -
_____

Put a 1 in each little box for your answer.
Add up your answers.
Write the total in this big box.

Verbs: Section 2
Summary 3-2

Circle the Word

Circle the correct word in the sentence.

1. We are (eating, ate) at the restaurant.

2. I (brought, bringing) a present to the party.

3. Susi (feed, fed) the fish yesterday.

4. Today I am (sleeping, slept) late.

5. I am (wore, wearing) a hat today.

6. Who (break, broke) this glass?

7. My sister (sweep, swept) the floor yesterday.

8. She is (shaking, shook) the dust out of the rug.

9. She (sat, sit) in my chair last night.

10. Who (taking, took) my book?

Put a 1 in each little box for your answer.
Add up your answers.
Write the total in this big box.

Name: _____

Progress Chart 2

Worksheet Number	Verbs	Date	Questions Completed	Total Possible
13.	found			7
14.	ate			7
15.	sat			7
16.	took			7
Review 4				10
17.	broke			7
18.	drank			7
19.	shook			7
20.	wore			7
Review 5				10
21.	slept			7
22.	fed			7
23.	swept			7
24.	brought			7
Review 6				10
Summary 3				10
Summary 4				10

Shape Up Your Language

Part I: Verbs — Past Tense

Section 3

Pre/Post-Test Sheet 3 140
sang (25a/b)   Worksheet 25 141
                  Activity Sheet 25 144
studied (26a/b)   Worksheet 26 145
                  Activity Sheet 26 148
gave (27a/b)   Worksheet 27 149
                  Activity Sheet 27 152
drew (28a/b)   Worksheet 28 153
                  Activity Sheet 28 156
Review 7 157

ran (29a/b)   Worksheet 29 159
                  Game 3: Running-the-Track Game 162
rang (30a/b)   Worksheet 30 163
                  Activity Sheet 30 166
struck (31a/b)   Worksheet 31 169
                  Activity Sheet 31 172
rode (32a/b)   Worksheet 32 173
                  Activity Sheet 32 176
Review 8 177

made (33a/b)   Worksheet 33 179
                  Activity Sheet 33 182
shot (34a/b)   Worksheet 34 183
                  Activity Sheet 34 186
wrote (35a/b)   Worksheet 35 187
                  Activity Sheet 35 190
bought (36a/b)   Worksheet 36 191
                  Activity Sheet 36 195
Review 9 196

Picture Summary 3 198
Game 4: Win Points/Lose Points 200
Summary Worksheet 5: Writing Sentences 202
Summary Worksheet 6: Circle the Word 204
Progress Chart 3 205

Name: _____ **Date:** _____

Pre/Post-Test Sheet (Verbs: Section 4)

Make flashcards of pictures 37a/b through 48a/b. See page 1 of manual.

Pre-Test	Date: _____	correct	incorrect	Post-Test	Date: _____	correct	incorrect
25 sang				25 sang			
26 studied				26 studied			
27 gave				27 gave			
28 drew				28 drew			
29 ran				29 ran			
30 rang				30 rang			
31 struck				31 struck			
32 rode				32 rode			
33 made				33 made			
34 shot				34 shot			
35 wrote				35 wrote			
36 bought				36 bought			

Post-Test Objective: The student will achieve 85% accuracy (10 out of 12 words). Repeat entire section if objective is not met.

Verbs: Section 3
Pre/Post-Test Sheet 3

◯

△

is singing   sang

**1. Find the picture that matches.
Find the picture that matches.
Fill in the blank with the correct word:**

◯ The bird is singing.

△ The bird _____ .

sing

sang

2. Write and say:

is singing   sang

_____   _____

- - - - - - - - - -   - - - - - - - - - -

Verbs: Section 3
Worksheet 25-1 (sang)

3. Fill in and say:

Yesterday we _____ "Happy Birthday"
at the birthday party.

4. Answer the question. Write your sentence in the blank:

What songs did you sing yesterday?

_____
- - - - - - - - - - - - - - - - - - -
_____
_____
- - - - - - - - - - - - - - - - - - -
_____

5. Fill in the missing letters and say the word:

sing   sang

sin __   san __

si __ __   sa __ __

s __ __ __   s __ __ __

__ __ __ __   __ __ __ __

6. Write and say the word four times:

☐

sing   sang

_____   _____
– – – – – – – – – – – –   – – – – – – – – – – – –
_____   _____
_____   _____
– – – – – – – – – – – –   – – – – – – – – – – – –
_____   _____
_____   _____
– – – – – – – – – – – –   – – – – – – – – – – – –
_____   _____
_____   _____
– – – – – – – – – – – –   – – – – – – – – – – – –
_____   _____

**7. Study the two words below.
Then close your eyes and spell:**

☐

sing

sang

**Put a 1 in each little box for your answer.
Add up your answers.
Write the total in this big box.**

Verbs: Section 3
Worksheet 25-3 (sang)

Name: _____ **Date:** _____

Color the cake and candles.
Cut out the candles and paste them on the cake.

1. Sing a birthday song.
   What did you sing?
2. Sing your favorite song.
   What did you sing?

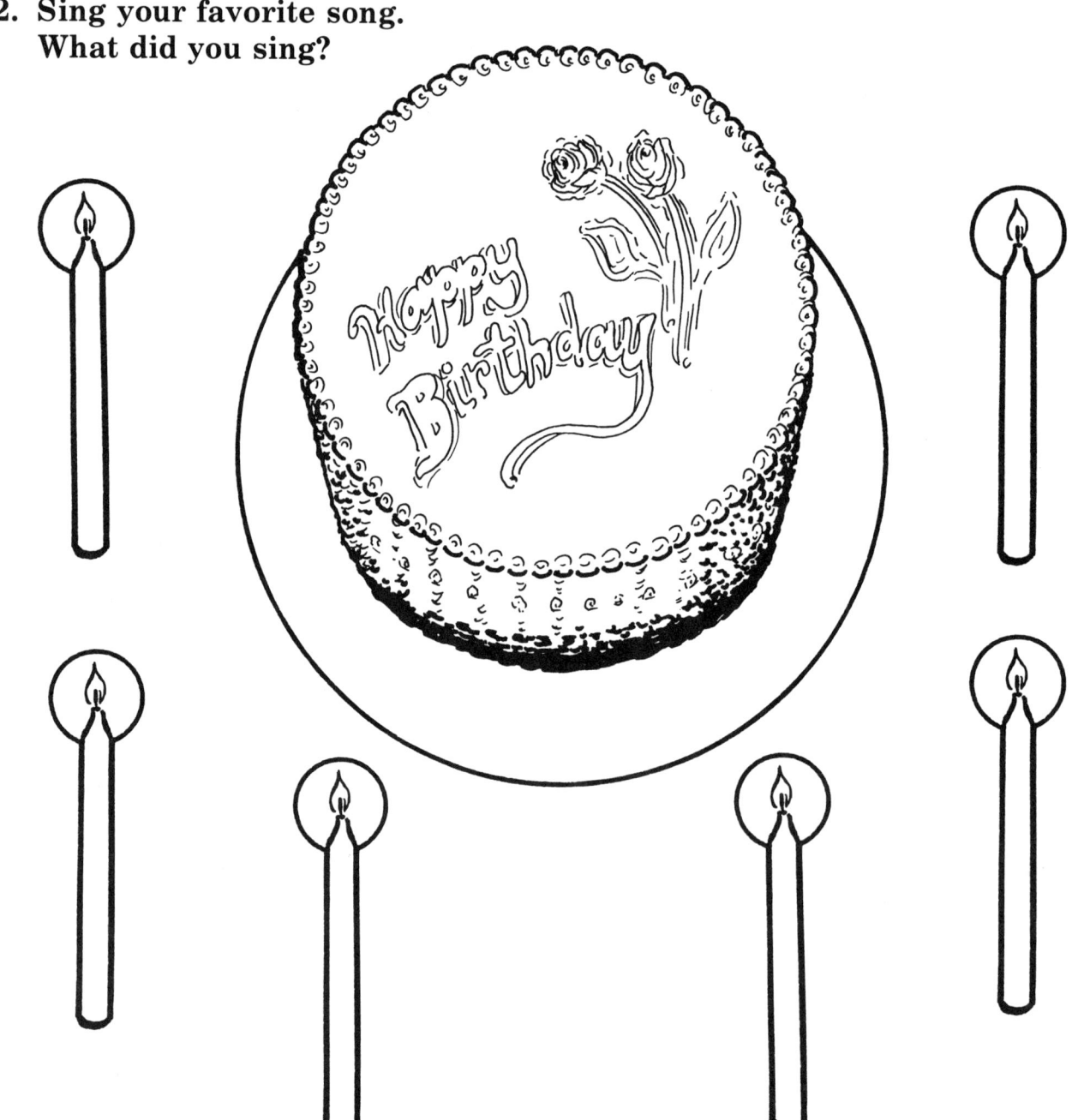

Verbs: Section 3
Activity Sheet 25 (sang)

○

△

is studying

studied

**1. Find the picture that matches.
   Fill in the blank with the correct word:**

○ The raccoon is studying.

△ The raccoon _____.

   studied

   study

2. Write and say:

is studying   studied

_ _ _ _ _ _ _ _ _   _ _ _ _ _ _ _ _ _ _ _

Verbs: Section 3
Worksheet 26-1 (studied)

3. Fill in and say:

Last night I _____ until 8 o'clock.

4. Answer the question. Write your sentence in the blank:

When did you study your spelling words?

_____

– – – – – – – – – – – – – – – –

_____
_____

– – – – – – – – – – – – – – – –

_____

5. Fill in the missing letters and say the word:

study   studied

stud __   studie __

stu __ __   studi __ __

st __ __ __   stud __ __ __

s __ __ __ __   stu __ __ __ __

__ __ __ __ __   st __ __ __ __ __

                               s __ __ __ __ __ __

                               __ __ __ __ __ __ __

6. **Write and say the word four times:**

study   studied

_____   _____

- - - - - - - - - - -   - - - - - - - - - - -
_____   _____
_____   _____

- - - - - - - - - - -   - - - - - - - - - - -
_____   _____

- - - - - - - - - - -   - - - - - - - - - - -
_____   _____

- - - - - - - - - - -   - - - - - - - - - - -
_____   _____

7. **Study the two words below.**
   Then close your eyes and spell:

study

studied

Put a 1 in each little box for your answer.
Add up your answers.
Write the total in this big box.

Name: _____ **Date:** _____

Write the name of a subject you are studying on the cover of the book.
Color and cut out the book.

1. What are you studying?
2. What did you study last week?

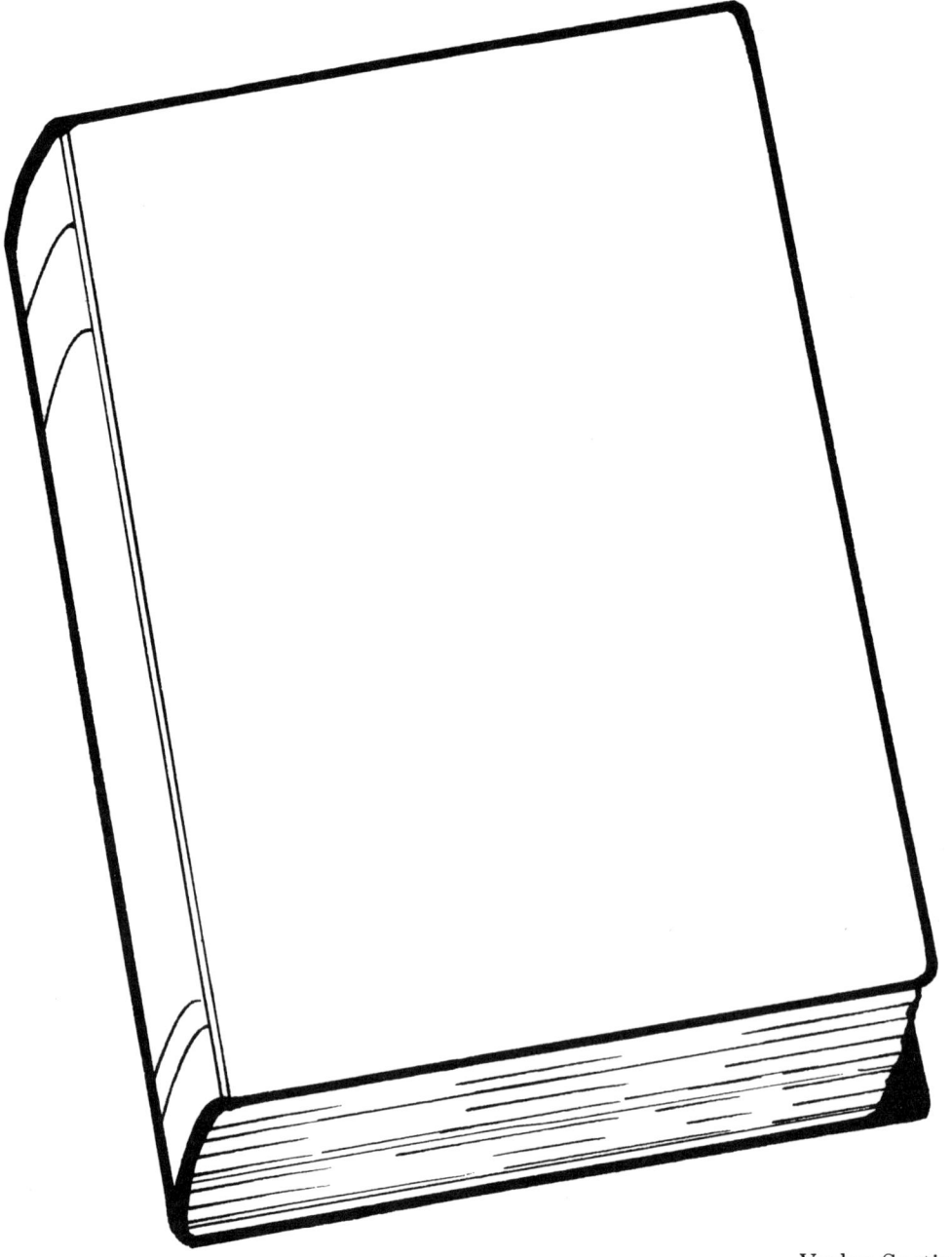

◯

△

is giving

gave

1. Find the picture that matches.
   Fill in the blank with the correct word:

◯ The bear is giving a present.

△ The bear _____ a present.

gave

give

2. Write and say:

is giving

gave

_____   _____

– – – – – – – – – – – – – –   – – – – – – – – – – – – – –

_____   _____

Verbs: Section 3
Worksheet 27-1 (gave)

3. Fill in and say:

Yesterday she _____ the dog a bone.

4. Answer the question. Write your sentence in the blank:

What did you give your friend for a birthday present?

_____

- -

_____

- -

_____

5. Fill in the missing letters and say the word:

give   gave

giv __   gav __

gi __ __   ga __ __

g __ __ __   g __ __ __

__ __ __ __   __ __ __ __

Verbs: Section 3
Worksheet 27-2 (gave)

6. Write and say the word four times:

give   gave

‾‾‾‾‾‾‾‾‾‾‾‾‾‾‾‾‾‾‾‾‾‾   ‾‾‾‾‾‾‾‾‾‾‾‾‾‾‾‾‾‾‾‾‾‾
- - - - - - - - - - - - - - -   - - - - - - - - - - - - - - -

‾‾‾‾‾‾‾‾‾‾‾‾‾‾‾‾‾‾‾‾‾‾   ‾‾‾‾‾‾‾‾‾‾‾‾‾‾‾‾‾‾‾‾‾‾
- - - - - - - - - - - - - - -   - - - - - - - - - - - - - - -

‾‾‾‾‾‾‾‾‾‾‾‾‾‾‾‾‾‾‾‾‾‾   ‾‾‾‾‾‾‾‾‾‾‾‾‾‾‾‾‾‾‾‾‾‾
- - - - - - - - - - - - - - -   - - - - - - - - - - - - - - -

‾‾‾‾‾‾‾‾‾‾‾‾‾‾‾‾‾‾‾‾‾‾   ‾‾‾‾‾‾‾‾‾‾‾‾‾‾‾‾‾‾‾‾‾‾
- - - - - - - - - - - - - - -   - - - - - - - - - - - - - - -

7. Study the two words below.
Then close your eyes and spell:

give

gave

Put a 1 in each little box for your answer.
Add up your answers.
Write the total in this big box.

Verbs: Section 3
Worksheet 27-3 (gave)

Name: _____ Date: _____

Color and cut out the foods.
Paste them on or around the plate.
Give the food to a person near you.

1. What are you doing?
2. What did you do?

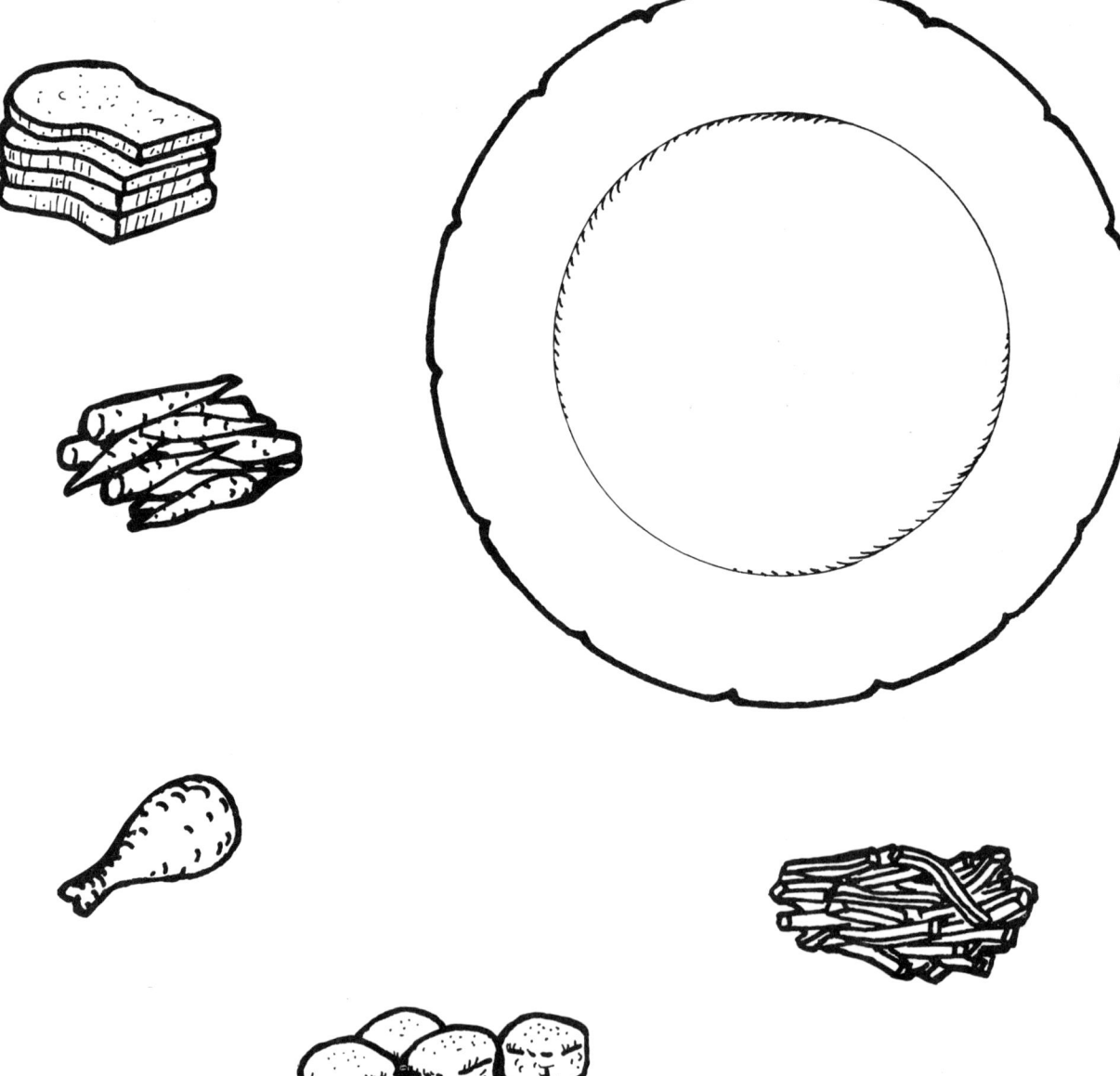

152

Verbs: Section 3
Activity Sheet 27 (gave)

Name: _____   **Date:** _____

       ○ is drawing   △  drew

1. Find the picture that matches.
Fill in the blank with the correct word:

○ The monkey is drawing.

△ The monkey _____.

     drew

     draw

2. Write and say:

   is drawing   drew

_____   _____

- - - - - - - - - - - - -   - - - - - - - - - - - - -

Verbs: Section 3
Worksheet 28-1 (drew)

Name: _____ **Date:** _____

3. Fill in and say:

Yesterday I _____ a picture of a tree.

4. Answer the question. Write your sentence in the blank:

What is the last thing you drew?

_____

_ _

_____

_____

_ _

_____

5. Fill in the missing letters and say the word:

draw	drew
dra __	dre __
dr __ __	dr __ __
d __ __ __	d __ __ __
__ __ __ __	__ __ __ __

Verbs: Section 3
Worksheet 28-2 (drew)

Name: _____ **Date:** _____

6. Write and say the word four times:

draw   drew

_____   _____
- - - - - - - - - - - - - - - -   - - - - - - - - - - - - - - - -
_____   _____
- - - - - - - - - - - - - - - -   - - - - - - - - - - - - - - - -
_____   _____
- - - - - - - - - - - - - - - -   - - - - - - - - - - - - - - - -
_____   _____
- - - - - - - - - - - - - - - -   - - - - - - - - - - - - - - - -

7. Study the two words below.
Then close your eyes and spell:

draw

drew

Put a 1 in each little box for your answer.
Add up your answers.
Write the total in this big box.

Name: _____ **Date:** _____

Draw a picture in the frame.

1. What are you drawing?

2. What did you draw?

Verbs: Section 3
Activity Sheet 28 (drew)

Name: _____ **Date:** _____

Fill in the blank with the correct word.
Then say the complete sentence:

1. Yesterday the bird sang a song.

   Today the bird _____ a song.

   sing

   is singing ☐

2. Now the monkey is drawing a picture.

   Yesterday the monkey _____ a picture.

   drew

   draw ☐

3. Yesterday the bear pushed the car.

   Now the bear _____ the car.

   is pushing

   pushed ☐

4. Today the raccoon is studying math.

   Yesterday the raccoon _____ math.

   is studying

   studied ☐

5. Yesterday the bear gave a present.

   Now the bear _____ a present.

   is giving

   give ☐

Verbs: Section 3
Review 7-1

6. Now the bird is singing a song.

   Yesterday the bird _____ a song.

   sing

   sang

   ☐

7. Yesterday the monkey drew a picture.

   Now the monkey _____ a picture.

   draw

   is drawing

   ☐

8. Now the bear is pushing the car.

   Yesterday the bear _____ the car.

   push

   pushed

   ☐

9. Yesterday the raccoon studied math.

   Today the raccoon _____ math.

   is studying

   read

   ☐

10. Now the bear is giving a present.

    Yesterday the bear _____ a present.

    give

    gave

    ☐

Put a 1 in each little box for your answer.
Add up your answers.
Write the total in this big box.

Verbs: Section 3
Review 7-2

Name: _____   **Date:** _____

○   △

is running   ran

1. Find the picture that matches.
    Fill in the blank with the correct word:

○   The raccoon is running.

△   The raccoon _____.

     ran

     run

2. Write and say:

is running   ran

_____   _____

\- \- \- \- \- \- \- \-   \- \- \- \- \- \- \- \-

_____   _____

Verbs: Section 3
Worksheet 29-1 (ran)

3. Fill in and say:

Yesterday the boy _____ around the playground.

4. Answer the question. Write your sentence in the blank:

Why did you run yesterday?

_____

- -

_____
_____

- -
_____

5. Fill in the missing letters and say the word:

run   ran

ru __   ra __

r __ __   r __ __

__ __ __   __ __ __

Verbs: Section 3
Worksheet 29-2 (ran)

6. **Write and say the word four times:**

run   ran

```
_____          _____
- - - - - - - - - -          - - - - - - - - - -
_____          _____
- - - - - - - - - -          - - - - - - - - - -
_____          _____
- - - - - - - - - -          - - - - - - - - - -
_____          _____
- - - - - - - - - -          - - - - - - - - - -
```

7. **Study the two words below.**
Then close your eyes and spell:

run

ran

Put a 1 in each little box for your answer.
Add up your answers.
Write the total in this big box.

Verbs: Section 3
Worksheet 29-3 (ran)

Running-the-Track Game (for 2 players)

1. Color each boy a different color and cut out the boys.
2. Each player chooses a boy.
3. The first player rolls a die and moves the boy the number of spaces indicated by the die.
4. The player then says how many spaces the boy ran.
5. The players take turns rolling the die and moving the boys.
6. The first boy across the finish line wins.

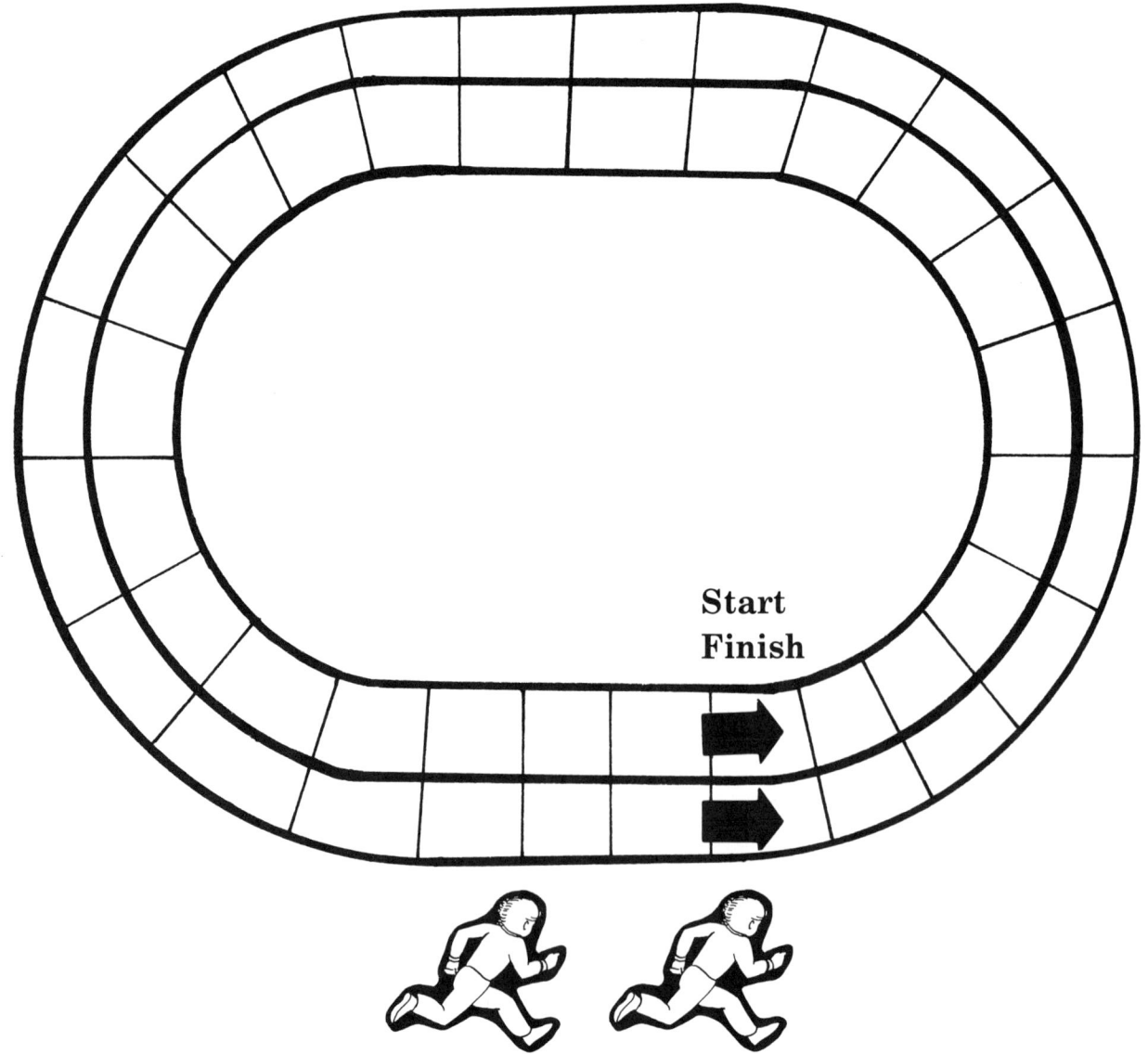

Start
Finish

Verbs: Section 3
Game 3 (ran)

Name: _____ **Date:** _____

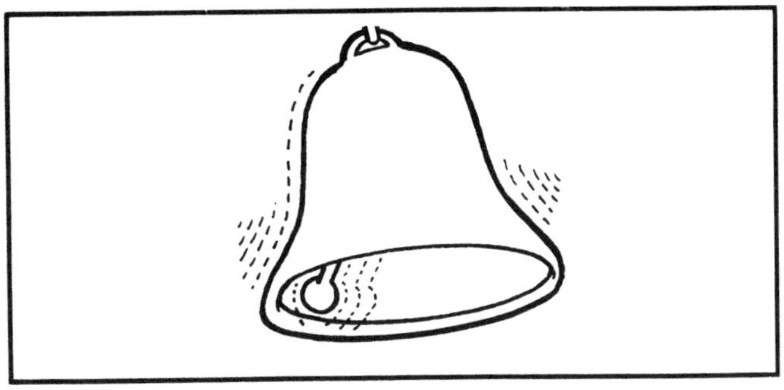

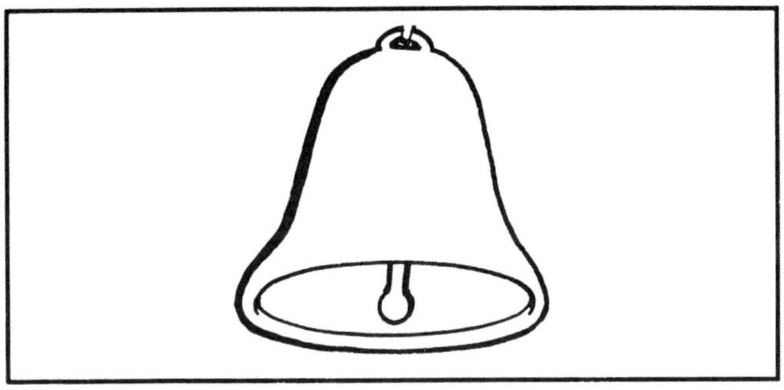

is ringing   rang

1. **Find the picture that matches.**
   Fill in the blank with the correct word:

○ The bell is ringing.

△ The bell _____.

   rang

   ring

2. **Write and say:**

   is ringing   rang

   _____   _____

   _____   _____

   _____   _____

Verbs: Section 3
Worksheet 30-1 (rang)

3. **Fill in and say:**

The phone _____ this morning.

4. **Answer the question. Write your sentence in the blank:**

When did the school bell ring?

_____
- - - - - - - - - - - - - - - - - -
=================================
_____
- - - - - - - - - - - - - - - - - -
_____

5. **Fill in the missing letters and say the word:**

ring   rang

rin __   ran __

ri __ __   ra __ __

r __ __ __   r __ __ __

__ __ __ __   __ __ __ __

6. Write and say the word four times:

ring   rang

⬜

_____   _____
- - - - - - - - - - - - -   - - - - - - - - - - - - -
━━━━━━━━━━━━━━━   ━━━━━━━━━━━━━━━
- - - - - - - - - - - - -   - - - - - - - - - - - - -
━━━━━━━━━━━━━━━   ━━━━━━━━━━━━━━━
- - - - - - - - - - - - -   - - - - - - - - - - - - -
━━━━━━━━━━━━━━━   ━━━━━━━━━━━━━━━
- - - - - - - - - - - - -   - - - - - - - - - - - - -
━━━━━━━━━━━━━━━   ━━━━━━━━━━━━━━━

7. Study the two words below.
Then close your eyes and spell:

⬜

ring

rang

Put a 1 in each little box for your answer.
Add up your answers.
Write the total in this big box.

Name: _____ Date: _____

Color and cut out the telephones and the doorbell.
Punch out holes in the telephones and receivers. Attach them with yarn.

Pick a partner.
Dial a number or ring the doorbell.
Your partner says, "The phone rang" or "The doorbell rang," and answers the phone or the door.
Have a conversation with your partner.
Take turns being the caller.

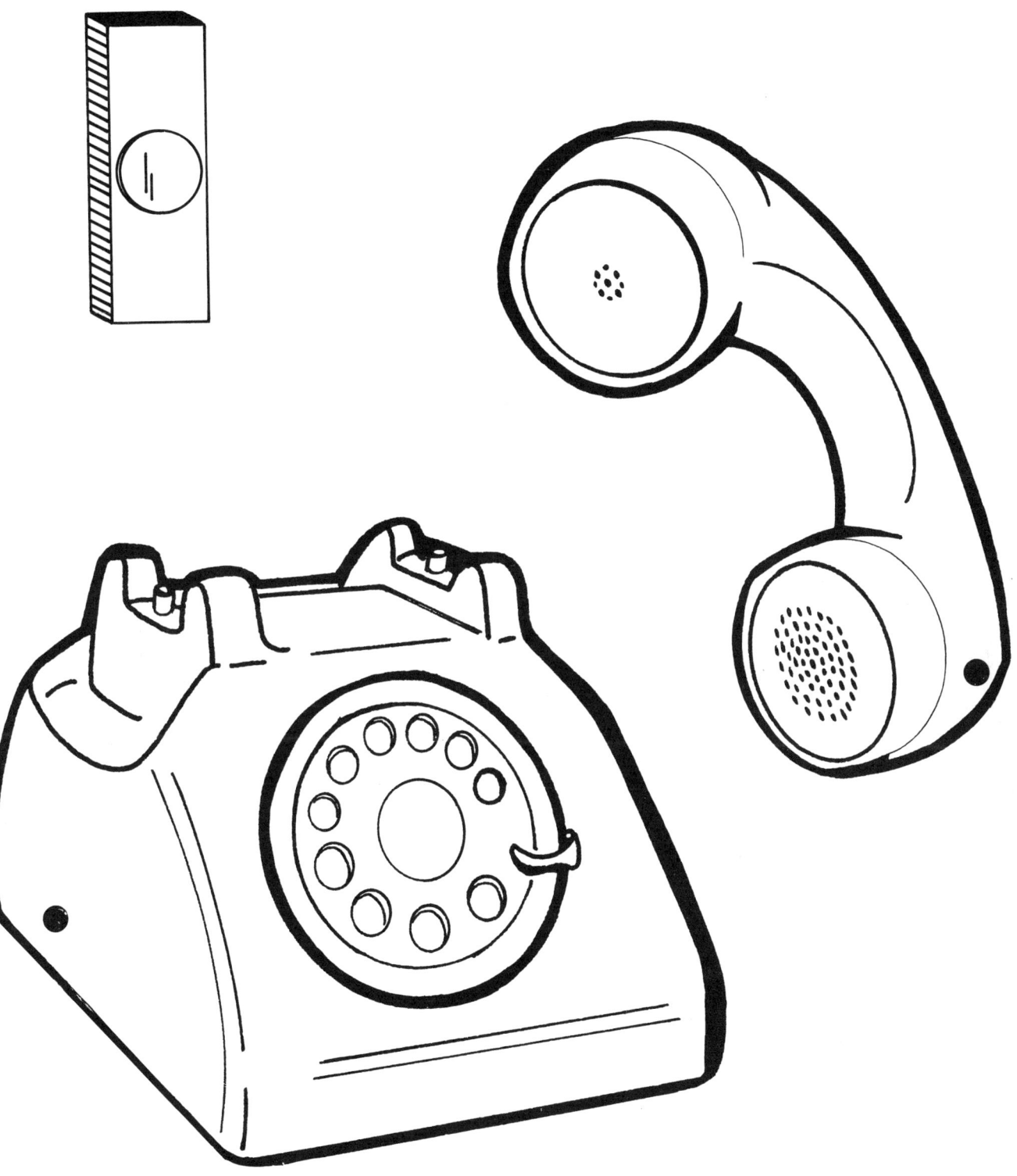

Verbs: Section 3
Activity Sheet 30-2 (rang)

◯

△

is striking

struck

1. **Find the picture that matches.**
   Fill in the blank with the correct word:

◯ The rabbit is striking the ball.

△ The rabbit _____ the ball.

strike

struck

2. **Write and say:**

is striking

struck

_____

_ _ _ _ _ _ _ _ _ _ _ _ _

_____

_ _ _ _ _ _ _ _ _ _ _ _ _

Verbs: Section 3
Worksheet 31-1 (struck)

3. Fill in and say:

Yesterday lightning _____ the tree.

4. Answer the question. Write your sentence in the blank:

Did you strike the ball with the bat when you played baseball?

_____

- -

_____
_____

- -

5. Fill in the missing letters and say the word:

strike	struck
strik __	struc __
stri __ __	stru __ __
str __ __ __	str __ __ __
st __ __ __ __	st __ __ __ __
s __ __ __ __ __	s __ __ __ __ __
__ __ __ __ __ __	__ __ __ __ __ __

6. Write and say the word four times:

strike   struck

---

7. Study the two words below.
Then close your eyes and spell:

strike

struck

Put a 1 in each little box for your answer.
Add up your answers.
Write the total in this big box.

Name: _____ Date: _____

Let's play paper croquet!
Color and cut out the mallet.
Paste or tape the mallet onto a pencil.
Make a ball out of cotton or crumple a two-inch square of paper.
Strike the ball so it follows the dotted lines.

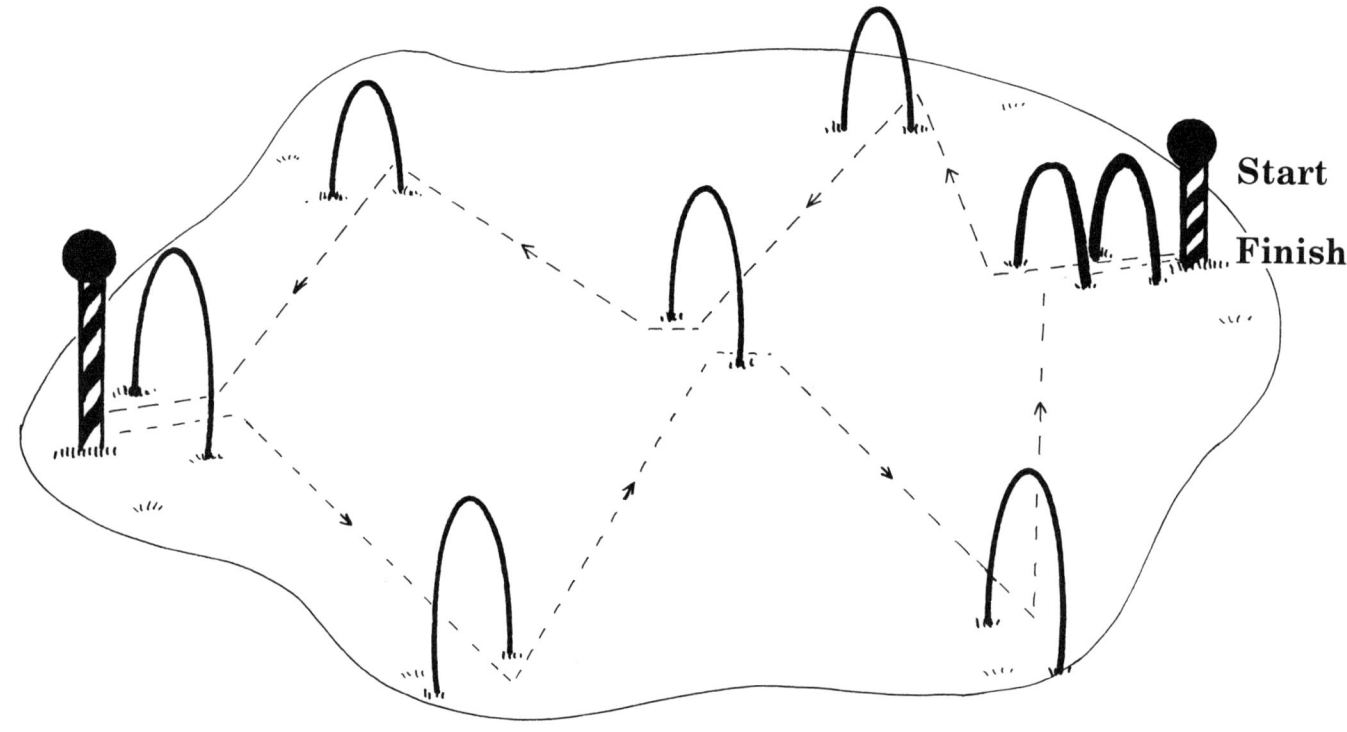

Start

Finish

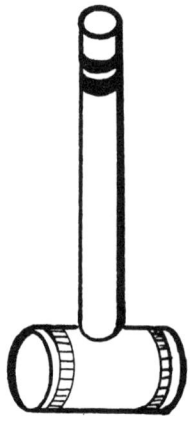

Verbs: Section 3
Activity Sheet 31 (struck)

Name: _____ **Date:** _____

○

△

is riding   rode

1. **Find the picture that matches.**
   Fill in the blank with the correct word:

   ○ The dog is riding the horse.

   △ The dog _____ the horse.

   rode

   ride

2. **Write and say:**

   is riding   rode

   _____   _____
   - - - - - - - - - -   - - - - - - - - - -
   _____   _____

Verbs: Section 3
Worksheet 32-1 (rode)

3. Fill in and say:

Yesterday we _____ the horses.

4. Answer the question. Write your sentence in the blank:

Where did you ride your bike?

_____

- -
_____
_____
- -
_____

5. Fill in the missing letters and say the word:

ride   rode

rid __   rod __

ri __ __   ro __ __

r __ __ __   r __ __ __

__ __ __ __   __ __ __ __

Verbs: Section 3
Worksheet 32-2 (rode)

Name: _____ Date: _____

6. Write and say the word four times:

ride   rode

7. Study the two words below.
Then close your eyes and spell:

ride

rode

Put a 1 in each little box for your answer.
Add up your answers.
Write the total in this big box.

Name: _____ **Date:** _____

Color and cut out the boy and the animals.
Make the boy ride each of the animals.

1. What is the boy doing?
2. What did he do?
3. Did you ever ride an animal?

Verbs: Section 3
Activity Sheet 32 (rode)

Name: _____ **Date:** _____

Fill in the blank with the correct word.
Then say the complete sentence:

1. Yesterday the dog rode the horse.

   Today the dog _____ the horse.

   ride

   is riding

2. Now the bell is ringing.

   Yesterday the bell _____.

   rang

   ring

3. Yesterday the raccoon closed the cage.

   Now the raccoon _____ the cage.

   close

   is closing

4. Now the rabbit is striking the baseball.

   Yesterday the rabbit _____ the baseball.

   struck

   is striking

5. Yesterday the raccoon ran.

   Today the raccoon _____.

   is running

   run

Verbs: Section 3
Review 8-1

6. Now the dog is riding the horse.

   Yesterday the dog _____ the horse.

   rode

   ride

7. Yesterday the bell rang.

   Today the bell _____.

   ring

   is ringing

8. Now the raccoon is closing the cage.

   Yesterday the raccoon _____ the cage.

   closed

   close

9. Yesterday the rabbit struck the baseball.

   Now the rabbit _____ the baseball.

   is striking

   struck

10. Today the raccoon is running.

    Yesterday the raccoon _____.

    run

    ran

Put a 1 in each little box for your answer.
Add up your answers.
Write the total in this big box.

◯   △

is making   made

1. **Find the picture that matches.**
   Fill in the blank with the correct word:

◯ The squirrel is making paper dolls.

△ The squirrel _____ paper dolls.

make

made

2. **Write and say:**

is making   made

_____   _____

– – – – – – – – –   – – – – – – – – –

_____   _____

Verbs: Section 3
Worksheet 33-1 (made)

3. Fill in and say:

Yesterday I _____ cookies.

4. Answer the question. Write your sentence in the blank:

What did you make last week?

-- -- -- -- -- -- -- -- -- -- -- -- -- -- --

==

-- -- -- -- -- -- -- -- -- -- -- -- -- -- --

==

5. Fill in the missing letters and say the word:

make   made

mak __   mad __

ma __ __   ma __ __

m __ __ __   m __ __ __

__ __ __ __   __ __ __ __

Verbs: Section 3
Worksheet 33-2 (made)

6. **Write and say the word four times:**

make   made

7. **Study the two words below.**
    Then close your eyes and spell:

make

made

Put a 1 in each little box for your answer.
Add up your answers.
Write the total in this big box.

Verbs: Section 3
Worksheet 33-3 (made)

To make a tiny paper hat, cut out the rectangle.
Fold on the dotted lines.

1. What are you making?
2. What did you make?

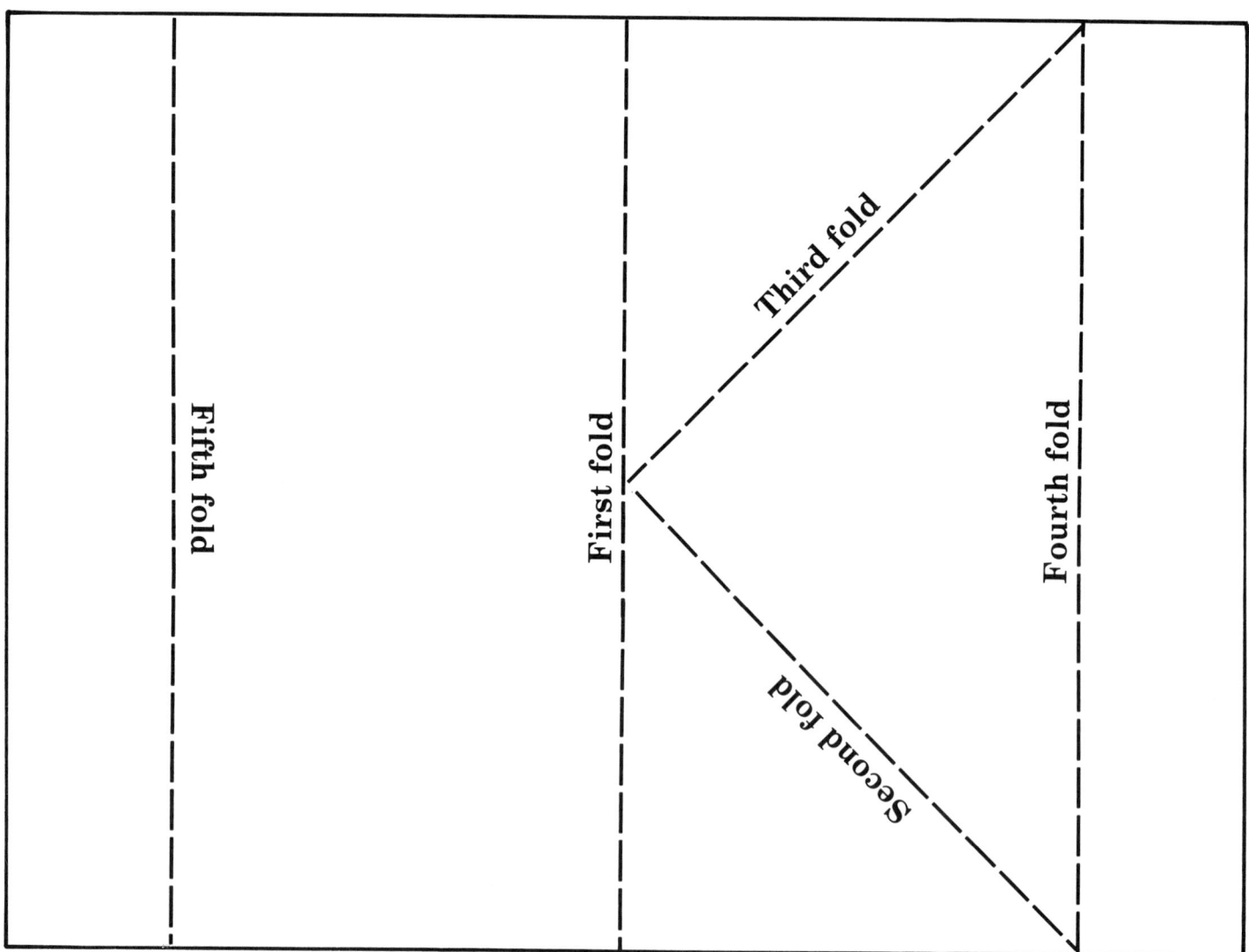

Verbs: Section 3
Activity Sheet 33 (made)

Name: _____   **Date:** _____

is shooting   shot

1. **Find the picture that matches.**
   Fill in the blank with the correct word:

○ The pig is shooting the basketball.

△ The pig _____ the basketball.

shoot

shot

2. **Write and say:**

shoot   shot

_____   _____

_ _ _ _ _ _ _ _ _   _ _ _ _ _ _ _ _ _

_____   _____

Verbs: Section 3
Worksheet 34-1 (shot)

3. Fill in and say:

Yesterday I _____ the basketball.

4. Answer the question. Write your sentence in the blank:

When did you last shoot a basketball?

5. Fill in the missing letters and say the word:

shoot   shot

shoo __   sho __

sho __ __   sh __ __

sh __ __ __   s __ __ __

s __ __ __ __   __ __ __ __

__ __ __ __ __

6. Write and say the word four times:

shoot   shot

‑‑‑‑‑‑‑‑‑‑‑‑‑‑‑‑‑‑‑‑‑‑‑‑‑‑‑   ‑‑‑‑‑‑‑‑‑‑‑‑‑‑‑‑‑‑‑‑‑‑‑‑‑‑‑

‑‑‑‑‑‑‑‑‑‑‑‑‑‑‑‑‑‑‑‑‑‑‑‑‑‑‑   ‑‑‑‑‑‑‑‑‑‑‑‑‑‑‑‑‑‑‑‑‑‑‑‑‑‑‑

‑‑‑‑‑‑‑‑‑‑‑‑‑‑‑‑‑‑‑‑‑‑‑‑‑‑‑   ‑‑‑‑‑‑‑‑‑‑‑‑‑‑‑‑‑‑‑‑‑‑‑‑‑‑‑

‑‑‑‑‑‑‑‑‑‑‑‑‑‑‑‑‑‑‑‑‑‑‑‑‑‑‑   ‑‑‑‑‑‑‑‑‑‑‑‑‑‑‑‑‑‑‑‑‑‑‑‑‑‑‑

**7. Study the two words below.
    Then close your eyes and spell:**

shoot

shot

**Put a 1 in each little box for your answer.
Add up your answers.
Write the total in this big box.**

Verbs: Section 3
Worksheet 34-3 (shot)

Cut out the hoop.
Cut the center from the hoop and crumple it to make a ball.
Tape the hoop to the edge of the table or place it flat across two piles of books.
Shoot the ball throught the hoop.

1. What are you doing?
2. What did you do?
3. How many times did you shoot the ball through the hoop?

Verbs: Section 3
Activity Sheet 34 (shot)

Name: _____ **Date:** _____

is writing   wrote

1. Find the picture that matches.
Fill in the blank with the correct word:

◯ The bird is writing a letter.

△ The bird _____ a letter.

write

wrote

2. Write and say:

is writing   wrote

_____   _____

_ _ _ _ _ _ _ _ _   _ _ _ _ _ _ _ _ _

_____   _____

Verbs: Section 3
Worksheet 35-1 (wrote)

3. Fill in and say:

Yesterday I _____ a letter to you.

4. Answer the question. Write your sentence in the blank:

When did you write a letter?

_____

— — — — — — — — — — — — — — — — — — — —

_____
_____

— — — — — — — — — — — — — — — — — — — —
_____

5. Fill in the missing letters and say the word:

write   wrote

writ __   wrot __

wri __ __   wro __ __

wr __ __ __   wr __ __ __

w __ __ __ __   w __ __ __ __

__ __ __ __ __   __ __ __ __ __

Name: _____ **Date:** _____

6. Write and say the word four times:

write   wrote

‾‾‾‾‾‾‾‾‾‾‾‾‾‾‾‾‾‾‾‾‾‾
- - - - - - - - - - - -
‾‾‾‾‾‾‾‾‾‾‾‾‾‾‾‾‾‾‾‾‾‾
- - - - - - - - - - - -
‾‾‾‾‾‾‾‾‾‾‾‾‾‾‾‾‾‾‾‾‾‾
- - - - - - - - - - - -
‾‾‾‾‾‾‾‾‾‾‾‾‾‾‾‾‾‾‾‾‾‾

7. Study the two words below.
Then close your eyes and spell:

write

wrote

Put a 1 in each little box for your answer.
Add up your answers.
Write the total in this big box.

Name: _____ **Date:** _____

Write a list of the people and pets who live in your house.
Put an X beside the girls' names.
Put an O beside the boys' names.
Put a □ beside your parents' names.
Put a △ beside your pets' names.
Hide this paper.

1. What names did you write?
2. On the back of this sheet, write a note to your teacher about your family or your pets.
   What did you write about?

My Family and Pets

1. _____

2. _____

3. _____

4. _____

5. _____

6. _____

7. _____

8. _____

9. _____

10. _____

Verbs: Section 3
Activity Sheet 35 (wrote)

○   △

is buying   bought

1. **Find the picture that matches.**
    Fill in the blank with the correct word:

○   The kangaroo is buying bread.

△   The kangaroo _____ bread.

buy

bought

2. **Write and say:**

is buying   bought

_____   _____

- - - - - - - - - -   - - - - - - - - - -

_____   _____

Verbs: Section 3
Worksheet 36-1 (bought)

3. Fill in and say:

I _____ bread yesterday.

4. Answer the question. Write your sentence in the blank:

When did you buy ice cream?

_____

- -

_____

- -

_____

5. Fill in the missing letters and say the word:

buy   bought

bu __   bough __

b __ __   boug __ __

__ __ __   bou __ __ __

                            bo __ __ __ __

                            b __ __ __ __ __

                            __ __ __ __ __ __

Verbs: Section 3
Worksheet 36-2 (bought)

6. Write and say the word four times:

☐

buy   bought

_____   _____
- - - - - - - - - - - - - -   - - - - - - - - - - - - - -
_____   _____
_____   _____
- - - - - - - - - - - - - -   - - - - - - - - - - - - - -
_____   _____
_____   _____
- - - - - - - - - - - - - -   - - - - - - - - - - - - - -
_____   _____

**7. Study the two words below.
Then close your eyes and spell:**

☐

buy

bought

**Put a 1 in each little box for your answer.
Add up your answers.
Write the total in this big box.**

Name: _____ **Date:** _____

Draw a picture of yourself buying something.

1. What are you doing in the picture?
2. What did you buy?

Verbs: Section 3
Activity Sheet 36

Name: _____ **Date:** _____

Fill in the blank with the correct word.
Then say the complete sentence:

1. Yesterday the pig shot the basketball.

   Now the pig _____ the basketball.

   shoot

   is shooting

2. Today the monkey is adding numbers.

   Yesterday the monkey _____ numbers.

   added

   add

3. Yesterday the kangaroo bought bread.

   Today the kangaroo _____ bread.

   is buying

   buy

4. Now the bird is writing a letter.

   Yesterday the bird _____ a letter.

   write

   wrote

5. Yesterday the squirrel made paper dolls.

   Today the squirrel _____ paper dolls.

   is making

   make

Verbs: Section 3
Review 9-1

6. Yesterday the bird wrote a letter.

   Now the bird _____ a letter.

   write

   is writing ☐

7. Yesterday the monkey added numbers.

   Today the monkey _____ numbers.

   is adding

   add ☐

8. Now the pig is shooting the basketball.

   Yesterday the pig _____ the basketball.

   shoot

   shot ☐

9. Today the kangaroo is buying bread.

   Yesterday the kangaroo _____ bread.

   bought

   buy ☐

10. Today the squirrel is making paper dolls.

    Yesterday the squirrel _____ paper dolls.

    made

    is making ☐

Put a 1 in each little box for your answer.
Add up your answers.
Write the total in this big box.

Picture Summary

Teacher:

On the following page is a picture summary. Look at the picture with the student and discuss what all of the animals are doing. First use the present progressive tense.

is singing

is studying

is giving

is drawing

is running

is ringing

is striking

is riding

is making

is shooting

is writing

is buying

Then say, "This picture was taken yesterday. Tell me what each animal did." Encourage the student to use each of the 12 verbs covered in the section in the past tense.

Verbs: Section 3
Picture Summary 3-2

Win Points/Lose Points

Teacher:
1. Give each player a marker.
2. Have all the markers placed on START.
3. Players may move in any direction. Moves are determined by rolling a die.
4. The object of the game is to be the first player to collect 16 points. A player lands on a space containing a verb or on a space that wins or loses points.
5. If landing on a space containing a verb, the player must say the past tense form of that verb. Each correct response is worth one point. No points are earned for incorrect responses.
6. If a player lands on a lose-points space, the points are subtracted from the player's score. If a player lands in a win-points space, they are added to the score.
7. The game is over when one player accumulates 16 points.

Name: _____ **Date:** _____

Start

buying	ringing	win 2 points	making
drawing	win 1 point	running	singing
lose 1 point	writing	giving	striking
studying	win 3 points	riding	ringing
shooting	lose 1 point	drawing	singing
lose 1 point	running	buying	win 2 points
giving	writing	lose all points	making
ringing	riding	ringing	win 3 points

Verbs: Section 3
Game 4-2

Name: _____ **Date:** _____

Writing Sentences

Write a sentence for each of these words.

1. sang _____ ☐

2. rode _____ ☐

3. bought _____ ☐

4. made _____ ☐

5. drew _____ ☐

6. studied _____ ☐

Verbs: Section 3
Summary 5-1

7. struck

8. gave

9. shot

10. ran

Put a 1 in each little box for your answer.
Add up your answers.
Write the total in this big box.

Verbs: Section 3
Summary 5-2

Name: _____ **Date:** _____

Circle the Word

Circle the correct word in the sentence.

1. I am (drawing, drew) a picture for the art show. ☐

2. She (writing, wrote) me a long letter. ☐

3. The boys (bought, buying) a flashlight. ☐

4. The bell (ringing, rang) when school started. ☐

5. He is (strike, striking) the ball. ☐

6. I (riding, rode) the horse all day yesterday. ☐

7. She (making, made) a cake. ☐

8. Karen (write, wrote) a story. ☐

9. I (singing, sang) the song for you last night. ☐

10. My best friend (run, ran) over to my house. ☐

Put a 1 in each little box for your answer.
Add up your answers.
Write the total in this big box.

Verbs: Section 3
Summary 6

Name: _____

Progress Chart 3

Worksheet Number	Verbs	Date	Questions Completed	Total Possible
25.	sang			7
26.	studied			7
27.	gave			7
28.	drew			7
Review 7				10
29.	ran			7
30.	rang			7
31.	struck			7
32.	rode			7
Review 8				10
33.	made			7
34.	shot			7
35.	wrote			7
36.	bought			7
Review 9				10
Summary 5				10
Summary 6				10

Shape Up Your Language

Part I: Verbs — Past Tense

Section 4

Pre/Post-Test Sheet 4		208
fell (37a/b)	Worksheet 37	209
	Activity Sheet 37	212
caught (38a/b)	Worksheet 38	213
	Activity Sheet 38	216
threw (39a/b)	Worksheet 39	217
	Activity Sheet 39	220
built (40a/b)	Worksheet 40	221
	Activity Sheet 40	224
Review 10		225
dug (41a/b)	Worksheet 41	227
	Activity Sheet 41	230
flew (42a/b)	Worksheet 42	231
	Activity Sheet 42	234
blew (43a/b)	Worksheet 43	235
	Activity Sheet 43	238
swam (44a/b)	Worksheet 44	239
	Activity Sheet 44	242
Review 11		243
swung (45a/b)	Worksheet 45	245
	Activity Sheet 45	248
slid (46a/b)	Worksheet 46	249
	Activity Sheet 46	252
hid (47a/b)	Worksheet 47	253
	Activity Sheet 47	256
hung (48a/b)	Worksheet 48	257
	Activity Sheet 48	261
Review 12		262
Picture Summary 4		264
Game 5: Egg Game		266
Summary Worksheet 7: Writing Sentences		270
Summary Worksheet 8: Word Wheel		272
Progress Chart 4		273

Name: _____ **Date:** _____

Pre/Post-Test Sheet (Verbs: Section 3)

Make flashcards of pictures 25a/b through 36a/b. See page 1 of manual.

Pre-Test	Date: _____	correct	incorrect	Post-Test	Date: _____	correct	incorrect
37	fell			37	fell		
38	caught			38	caught		
39	threw			39	threw		
40	built			40	built		
41	dug			41	dug		
42	flew			42	flew		
43	blew			43	blew		
44	swam			44	swam		
45	swung			45	swung		
46	slid			46	slid		
47	hid			47	hid		
48	hung			48	hung		

Post-Test Objective: The student will achieve 85% accuracy (10 out of 12 words). Repeat entire section if objective is not met.

Verbs: Section 4
Pre/Post-Test Sheet 4

○

△

is falling

fell

1. Find the picture that matches.
Fill in the blank with the correct word:

○ The raccoon is falling from the tree.

△ The raccoon _____ from the tree.

fall

fell

2. Write and say:

is falling   fell

_____   _____

‒ ‒ ‒ ‒ ‒ ‒ ‒ ‒ ‒ ‒ ‒   ‒ ‒ ‒ ‒ ‒ ‒ ‒ ‒ ‒ ‒ ‒

_____   _____

Verbs: Section 4
Worksheet 37-1 (fell)

3. Fill in and say:

The apple _____ off the tree yesterday.

4. Answer the question. Write your sentence in the blank:

Where were you the last time you fell down?

_____

- -

_____
_____

- -

_____

5. Fill in the missing letters and say the word:

fall   fell

fal __   fel __

fa __ __   fe __ __

f __ __ __   f __ __ __

__ __ __ __   __ __ __ __

6. Write and say the word four times:

fall   fell

_____   _____
- - - - - - - - - - - - -   - - - - - - - - - - - - -
_____   _____

_____   _____
- - - - - - - - - - - - -   - - - - - - - - - - - - -
_____   _____

_____   _____
- - - - - - - - - - - - -   - - - - - - - - - - - - -
_____   _____

_____   _____
- - - - - - - - - - - - -   - - - - - - - - - - - - -
_____   _____

7. Study the two words below.
   Then close your eyes and spell:

fall

fell

Put a 1 in each little box for your answer.
Add up your answers.
Write the total in this big box.

Color and cut out the leaf.
Let it fall to the ground.

1. What did the leaf do?
2. Tell about the leaves falling off the trees in autumn.
3. Write the words *fall* and *fell* on the back of the leaf.

Name: _____ **Date:** _____

is catching   caught

1. **Find the picture that matches.**
   Fill in the blank with the correct word:

○ The monkey is catching the ball.

△ The monkey _____ the ball.
   caught
   catch

2. **Write and say:**

   is catching   caught

   _____   _____
   — — — — — — — — —   — — — — — — — — —
   _____   _____

Verbs: Section 4
Worksheet 38-1 (caught)

3. Fill in and say:

I _____ a cold.

4. Answer the question. Write your sentence in the blank:

When did you catch a cold?

_____

- -

_____
_____

- -

_____

5. Fill in the missing letters and say the word:

catch	caught
catc __	caugh __
cat __ __	caug __ __
ca __ __ __	cau __ __ __
c __ __ __ __	ca __ __ __ __
__ __ __ __ __	c __ __ __ __ __
	__ __ __ __ __ __

Name: _____ Date: _____

6. **Write and say the word four times:**

catch   caught

- - - - - - - - - - - - -   - - - - - - - - - - - - -

- - - - - - - - - - - - -   - - - - - - - - - - - - -

- - - - - - - - - - - - -   - - - - - - - - - - - - -
---

7. **Study the two words below.**
    Then close your eyes and spell:

catch

caught

Put a 1 in each little box for your answer.
Add up your answers.
Write the total in this big box.

Name: _____ **Date:** _____

Draw a ball for the boy to catch.

1. What is he doing?
2. What did he do?
3. Tell a story about playing baseball.

Verbs: Section 4
Activity Sheet 38 (caught)

◯

△

is throwing

threw

**1. Find the picture that matches.
Fill in the blank with the correct word:**

◯ The monkey is throwing the baseball.

△ The monkey _____ the baseball.

throw

threw

2. Write and say:

is throwing

threw

_____

_ _ _ _ _ _ _ _ _ _ _

_____

_____

_ _ _ _ _ _ _ _ _ _ _

_____

Verbs: Section 4
Worksheet 39-1 (threw)

3. Fill in and say:

Yesterday I _____ the trash in the wastebasket.

4. Answer the question. Write your sentence in the blank:

When did you throw away something important?

5. Fill in the missing letters and say the word:

throw	threw
thro __	thre __
thr __ __	thr __ __
th __ __ __	th __ __ __
t __ __ __ __	t __ __ __ __
__ __ __ __ __	__ __ __ __ __

Verbs: Section 4
Worksheet 39-2 (threw)

6. Write and say the word four times:

throw   threw

⬜

‒ ‒ ‒ ‒ ‒ ‒ ‒ ‒ ‒ ‒ ‒ ‒   ‒ ‒ ‒ ‒ ‒ ‒ ‒ ‒ ‒ ‒ ‒ ‒

‒ ‒ ‒ ‒ ‒ ‒ ‒ ‒ ‒ ‒ ‒ ‒   ‒ ‒ ‒ ‒ ‒ ‒ ‒ ‒ ‒ ‒ ‒ ‒

‒ ‒ ‒ ‒ ‒ ‒ ‒ ‒ ‒ ‒ ‒ ‒   ‒ ‒ ‒ ‒ ‒ ‒ ‒ ‒ ‒ ‒ ‒ ‒

‒ ‒ ‒ ‒ ‒ ‒ ‒ ‒ ‒ ‒ ‒ ‒   ‒ ‒ ‒ ‒ ‒ ‒ ‒ ‒ ‒ ‒ ‒ ‒

**7. Study the two words below.
     Then close your eyes and spell:**

⬜

throw

threw

Put a 1 in each little box for your answer.
Add up your answers.
Write the total in this big box.

Name: _____ **Date:** _____

Color and cut out the ball.
Write the words *throw* and *threw* on the back of the ball.
Crumple up the ball and throw it!

1. What did you do?
2. Where did you throw it?

Name: _____   **Date:** _____

○

△

is building   built

1. Find the picture that matches.
   Fill in the blank with the correct word:

○ The bear is building a sand castle.

△ The bear _____ a sand castle.

   build
   built

2. Write and say:

is building   built

_ _ _ _ _ _ _ _ _ _ _ _ _ _ _ _ _ _   _ _ _ _ _ _ _ _ _ _ _ _ _ _ _ _ _

Verbs: Section 4
Worksheet 40-1 (built)

3. Fill in and say:

Last year my dad _____ a clubhouse
for me.

4. Answer the question. Write your sentence in the blank:

What did you build last month?

_____
- - - - - - - - - - - - - - - - - - - -
=========================
_____
- - - - - - - - - - - - - - - - - - - -
=========================

5. Fill in the missing letters and say the word:

build   built

buil __   buil __

bui __ __   bui __ __

bu __ __ __   bu __ __ __

b __ __ __ __   b __ __ __ __

__ __ __ __ __   __ __ __ __ __

6. Write and say the word four times:

build   built

_____   _____
- - - - - - - - - - - - - - - - -   - - - - - - - - - - - - - - - - -
_____   _____
- - - - - - - - - - - - - - - - -   - - - - - - - - - - - - - - - - -
_____   _____
- - - - - - - - - - - - - - - - -   - - - - - - - - - - - - - - - - -
_____   _____
- - - - - - - - - - - - - - - - -   - - - - - - - - - - - - - - - - -
_____   _____

**7. Study the two words below.
    Then close your eyes and spell:**

build

built

**Put a 1 in each little box for your answer.
Add up your answers.
Write the total in this big box.**

Verbs: Section 4
Worksheet 40-3 (built)

Draw a hammer in the man's hand so he can build a doghouse.

1. What is the man doing?
2. What did he do?
3. Tell about something that you helped build.

Name: _____ **Date:** _____

Fill in the blank with the correct word.
Then say the complete sentence:

1. Yesterday I _____ a baseball.

   catch

   caught □

2. Now I _____ a glass of water.

   am drinking

   drank □

3. Yesterday he _____ into the pool.

   fell

   is falling □

4. Now she _____ a model airplane.

   built

   is building □

5. Yesterday I _____ a football.

   throw

   threw □

6. Now he _____ the baseball.

   catch

   is catching □

Verbs: Section 4
Review 10-1

7. Yesterday we _____ a glass of lemonade.

   drank

   drink

8. Yesterday he _____ a robot.

   build

   built

9. Now he _____ the football.

   is throwing

   throw

10. The cat _____ into the pool!

    fall

    is falling

Put a 1 in each little box for your answer.
Add up your answers.
Write the total in this big box.

Verbs: Section 4
Review 10-2

Name: _____ **Date:** _____

◯

△

is digging

dug

1. **Find the picture that matches.**
   Fill in the blank with the correct word:

   ◯ The pig is digging a hole.

   △ The pig _____ a hole.

   dig
   dug

2. **Write and say:**

   is digging

   dug

   _____

   _____

   _____

   _____

Verbs: Section 4
Worksheet 41-1 (dug)

Name: _____ Date: _____

3. Fill in and say:

Yesterday the dog _____ up a bone.

4. Answer the question. Write your sentence in the blank:

Where did you dig a hole?

_____

– –

_____
_____

– –

_____

5. Fill in the missing letters and say the word:

dig   dug

di __   du __

d __ __   d __ __

__ __ __   __ __ __

Verbs: Section 4
Worksheet 41-2 (dug)

6. **Write and say the word four times:**

dig   dug

_____   _____
- - - - - - - - - - - -   - - - - - - - - - - - -
_____   _____
_____   _____
- - - - - - - - - - - -   - - - - - - - - - - - -
_____   _____
_____   _____
- - - - - - - - - - - -   - - - - - - - - - - - -
_____   _____
_____   _____
- - - - - - - - - - - -   - - - - - - - - - - - -
_____   _____

7. **Study the two words below.**
Then close your eyes and spell:

dig

dug

Put a 1 in each little box for your answer.
Add up your answers.
Write the total in this big box.

Verbs: Section 4
Worksheet 41-3 (dug)

Name: _____ **Date:** _____

Draw a shovel for the girl to use.

1. What is she doing?
2. What did she do?
3. Tell a story about digging a hole.

Verbs: Section 4
Activity Sheet 41 (dug)

○   △

is flying   flew

1. Find the picture that matches.
   Fill in the blank with the correct word:

○ The rabbit is flying the kite.

△ The rabbit _____ the kite.

   flew
   fly

2. Write and say:

   is flying   flew

   _____   _____

   — — — — — — — —   — — — — — — — —

   _____   _____

231

Verbs: Section 4
Worksheet 42-1 (flew)

Name: _____ **Date:** _____

3. Fill in and say:

Yesterday the bird _____ out of
the nest.

4. Answer the question. Write your sentence in the blank:

Where did you fly a kite?

_____

- -
_____

- -
_____

5. Fill in the missing letters and say the word:

fly	flew
fl __	fle __
f __ __	fl __ __
__ __ __	f __ __ __
	__ __ __ __

Verbs: Section 4
Worksheet 42-2 (flew)

Name: _____ **Date:** _____

6. **Write and say the word four times:**

fly   flew

‾‾‾‾‾‾‾‾‾‾‾‾‾‾‾‾‾‾‾‾‾‾‾‾‾‾‾‾   ‾‾‾‾‾‾‾‾‾‾‾‾‾‾‾‾‾‾‾‾‾‾‾‾‾‾

- - - - - - - - - - - - - - - - -   - - - - - - - - - - - - - - - - -

‾‾‾‾‾‾‾‾‾‾‾‾‾‾‾‾‾‾‾‾‾‾‾‾‾‾‾‾   ‾‾‾‾‾‾‾‾‾‾‾‾‾‾‾‾‾‾‾‾‾‾‾‾‾‾

- - - - - - - - - - - - - - - - -   - - - - - - - - - - - - - - - - -

‾‾‾‾‾‾‾‾‾‾‾‾‾‾‾‾‾‾‾‾‾‾‾‾‾‾‾‾   ‾‾‾‾‾‾‾‾‾‾‾‾‾‾‾‾‾‾‾‾‾‾‾‾‾‾

- - - - - - - - - - - - - - - - -   - - - - - - - - - - - - - - - - -

‾‾‾‾‾‾‾‾‾‾‾‾‾‾‾‾‾‾‾‾‾‾‾‾‾‾‾‾   ‾‾‾‾‾‾‾‾‾‾‾‾‾‾‾‾‾‾‾‾‾‾‾‾‾‾

- - - - - - - - - - - - - - - - -   - - - - - - - - - - - - - - - - -

7. **Study the two words below.**
Then close your eyes and spell:

fly

flew

Put a 1 in each little box for your answer.
Add up your answers.
Write the total in this big box.

Name: _____ Date: _____

Cut out rectangle. Place on table print-side down.
Fold points A and B over to meet in center.
Fold in half so C meets D.
Fold lines E and F down.
Fold lines G and H down.
Now fly your paper airplane.

1. What are you doing?
2. What did you do?

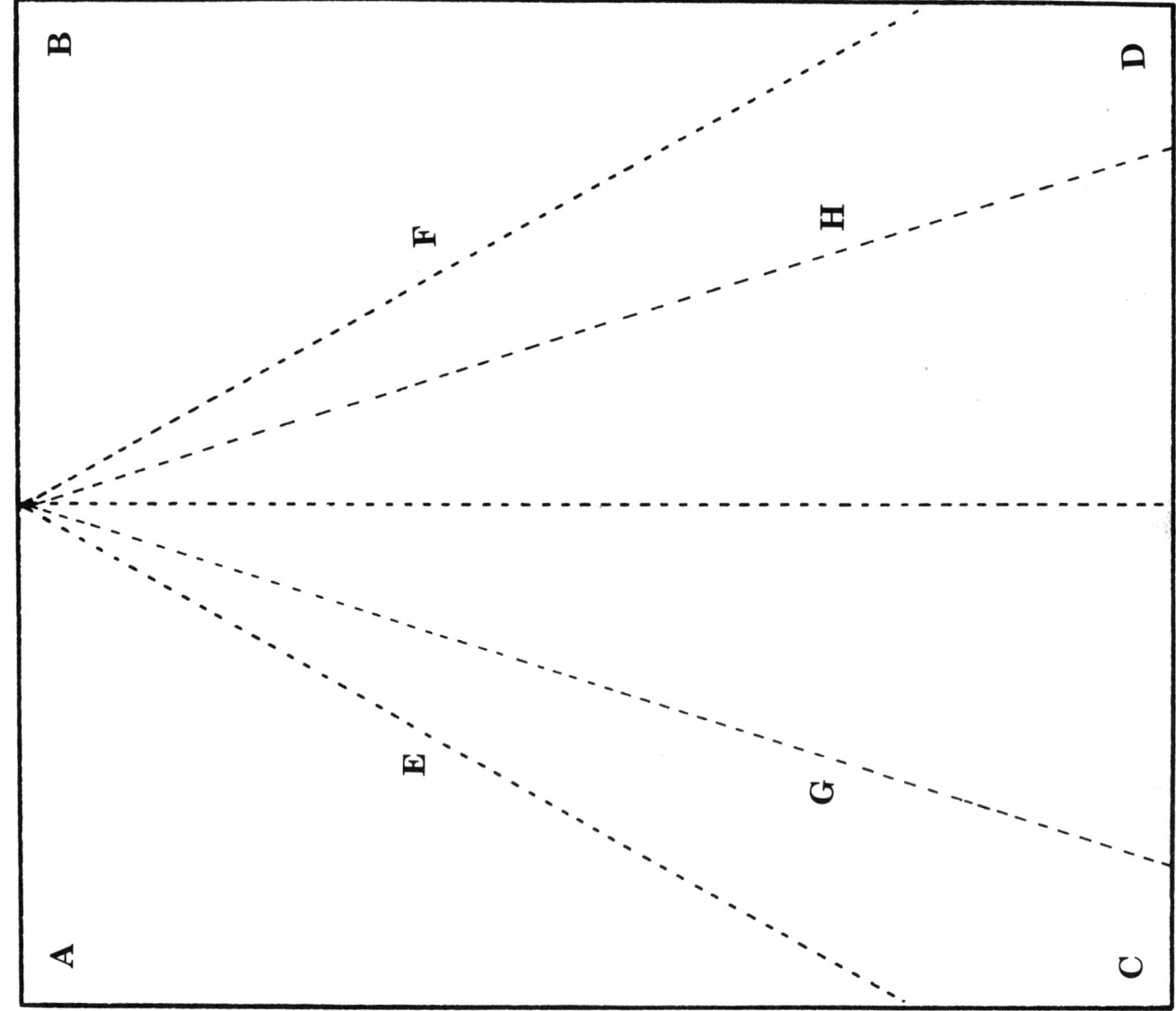

◯

△

is blowing

blew

1. Find the picture that matches.
Fill in the blank with the correct word:

◯ The kangaroo is blowing a bubble.

△ The kangaroo _____ bubbles.

blow

blew

2. Write and say:

is blowing

blew

_____

- - - - - - - - - -

_____

_____

- - - - - - - - - -

_____

Verbs: Section 4
Worksheet 43-1 (blew)

3. Fill in and say:

The wind _____ hard last night.

4. Answer the question. Write your sentence in the blank:

How many candles did you blow out on your birthday?

_____
- - - - - - - - - - - - - - - - - - - -
_____
_____
- - - - - - - - - - - - - - - - - - - -
_____

5. Fill in the missing letters and say the word:

blow   blew

blo __   ble __

bl __ __   bl __ __

b __ __ __   b __ __ __

__ __ __ __   __ __ __ __

6. Write and say the word four times:

blow   blew

_____   _____
- - - - - - - - - - - - - - - - -   - - - - - - - - - - - - - - - - -
_____   _____
- - - - - - - - - - - - - - - - -   - - - - - - - - - - - - - - - - -
_____   _____
- - - - - - - - - - - - - - - - -   - - - - - - - - - - - - - - - - -
_____   _____
- - - - - - - - - - - - - - - - -   - - - - - - - - - - - - - - - - -
_____   _____

**7. Study the two words below.
    Then close your eyes and spell:**

blow

blew

**Put a 1 in each little box for your answer.
Add up your answers.
Write the total in this big box.**

Verbs: Section 4
Worksheet 43-3 (blew)

Name: _____ **Date:** _____

Draw some bubbles.

1. What is the boy doing?
2. What did he do?
3. How many bubbles did he blow?

Verbs: Section 4
Activity Sheet 43 (blew)

Name: _____　　**Date:** _____

○

△

is swimming   swam

1. **Find the picture that matches.**
   Fill in the blank with the correct word:

○ The bear is swimming.

△ The bear _____.

swam

swim

2. **Write and say:**

is swimming   swam

_____   _____

- - - - - - - - - -   - - - - - - - - - -

_____   _____

Verbs: Section 4
Worksheet 44-1 (swam)

3. Fill in and say:

Yesterday the ducks _____ across the lake.

☐

4. Answer the question. Write your sentence in the blank:

Where did you swim last summer?

☐

‾‾‾‾‾‾‾‾‾‾‾‾‾‾‾‾‾‾‾‾‾‾‾‾‾‾‾‾‾‾‾‾‾‾‾‾

- - - - - - - - - - - - - - - - - - -

‾‾‾‾‾‾‾‾‾‾‾‾‾‾‾‾‾‾‾‾‾‾‾‾‾‾‾‾‾‾‾‾‾‾‾‾

- - - - - - - - - - - - - - - - - - -

‾‾‾‾‾‾‾‾‾‾‾‾‾‾‾‾‾‾‾‾‾‾‾‾‾‾‾‾‾‾‾‾‾‾‾‾

5. Fill in the missing letters and say the word:

☐

swim   swam

swi __   swa __

sw __ __   sw __ __

s __ __ __   s __ __ __

__ __ __ __   __ __ __ __

6. **Write and say the word four times:**

swim   swam

_____   _____
— — — — — — — — — — — —   — — — — — — — — — — — —
_____   _____
_____   _____
— — — — — — — — — — — —   — — — — — — — — — — — —
_____   _____
— — — — — — — — — — — —   — — — — — — — — — — — —
_____   _____
_____   _____
— — — — — — — — — — — —   — — — — — — — — — — — —
_____   _____

7. **Study the two words below.**
Then close your eyes and spell:

swim

swam

Put a 1 in each little box for your answer.
Add up your answers.
Write the total in this big box.

Color and cut out the duck and the pond.
Cut a slit on the dotted line in the pond.
Make the duck swim in the pond.

1. What is the duck doing?
2. Take him out of the water. What did he do?
3. Tell a story about a duck swimming in a lake.

Verbs: Section 4
Activity Sheet 44 (swam)

Name: _____ **Date:** _____

Fill in the blank with the correct word.
Then say the complete sentence:

1. Yesterday she _____ in the lake.

   swim

   swam   ☐

2. Now I _____ a bubble.

   blew

   am blowing   ☐

3. Yesterday he _____ a hole.

   dug

   am digging   ☐

4. Today I _____ the bell.

   ringing

   am ringing   ☐

5. Yesterday I _____ a kite.

   am flying

   flew   ☐

6. Right now my sister _____.

   swam

   is swimming   ☐

Verbs: Section 4
Review 11-1

7. Yesterday the baby _____ some bubbles.

 blow

 blew

☐

8. Now the dog _____ a hole.

 is digging

 dig

☐

9. Yesterday my friend _____ the bell.

 rang

 is ringing

☐

10. Now my friend _____ a kite.

 fly

 is flying

☐

Put a 1 in each little box for your answer.
Add up your answers.
Write the total in this big box.

○

△

is swinging    swung

1. **Find the picture that matches.**
   Fill in the blank with the correct word:

○ The raccoon is swinging.

△ The raccoon _____ .

swing

swung

2. **Write and say:**

is swinging   swung

_____   _____

_____   _____

Verbs: Section 4
Worksheet 45-1 (swung)

3. Fill in and say:

Yesterday the monkey _____ in the tree.

4. Answer the question. Write your sentence in the blank:

When did you swing at the playground?

_____

- -
_____
_____
- -
_____

5. Fill in the missing letters and say the word:

swing   swung

swin __   swun __

swi __ __   swu __ __

sw __ __ __   sw __ __ __

s __ __ __ __   s __ __ __ __

__ __ __ __ __   __ __ __ __ __

6. Write and say the word four times:

swing   swung

7. Study the two words below.
Then close your eyes and spell:

swing

swung

Put a 1 in each little box for your answer.
Add up your answers.
Write the total in this big box.

Verbs: Section 4
Worksheet 45-3 (swung)

Name: _____ **Date:** _____

Draw a girl in one of the swings.
Draw a boy walking away from the swings.

1. What is the girl doing?
2. What did the boy do?
3. Tell a story about playing on the playground.

Verbs: Section 4
Activity Sheet 45 (swung)

◯

△

is sliding

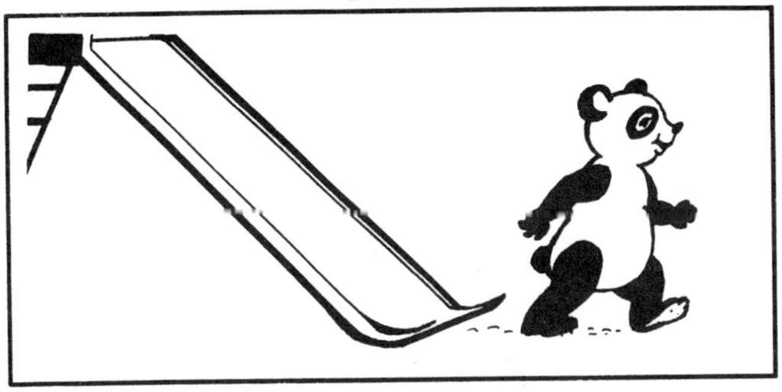

slid

1. Find the picture that matches.
   Fill in the blank with the correct word: ⬚

◯ The bear is sliding.

△ The bear _____.

slide

slid

2. Write and say: ⬚

is sliding

slid

_____

– – – – – – – – – –

_____

– – – – – – – – – –

Verbs: Section 4
Worksheet 46-1 (slid)

3. Fill in and say:

Yesterday the car _____ on the wet street.

4. Answer the question. Write your sentence in the blank:

When did you slide at the playground?

_____

- - - - - - - - - - - - - - - - - - -

_____
_____

- - - - - - - - - - - - - - - - - - -

_____

5. Fill in the missing letters and say the word:

slide   slid

slid __   sli __

sli __ __   sl __ __

sl __ __ __   s __ __ __

s __ __ __ __   __ __ __ __

__ __ __ __ __

6. Write and say the word four times:

slide   slid

_____

- - - - - - - - - - - -   - - - - - - - - - - - -
_____   _____
_____   _____

- - - - - - - - - - - -   - - - - - - - - - - - -
_____   _____

- - - - - - - - - - - -   - - - - - - - - - - - -
_____   _____

- - - - - - - - - - - -   - - - - - - - - - - - -

**7. Study the two words below.
Then close your eyes and spell:**

slide

slid

**Put a 1 in each little box for your answer.
Add up your answers.
Write the total in this big box.**

Verbs: Section 4
Worksheet 46-3 (slid)

Color and cut out the girl.
Make the girl slide down the slide.

1. What is she doing?
2. What did she do?
3. How many times did she slide?

Verbs: Section 4
Activity Sheet 46 (slid)

○

△

is hiding

hid

1. **Find the picture that matches.**
   Fill in the blank with the correct word:

○ The pig is hiding.

△ The pig _____.

   hide
   hid

2. **Write and say:**

   is hiding   hid

   _____   _____
   _ _ _ _ _ _ _ _ _   _ _ _ _ _ _ _ _ _
   _____   _____

Verbs: Section 4
Worksheet 47-1 (hid)

3. Fill in and say:

Yesterday my mom _____ the candy.

4. Answer the question. Write your sentence in the blank:

Where did you hide the last time you played Hide and Seek?

_____

- - - - - - - - - - - - - - - - - - -

_____
_____

- - - - - - - - - - - - - - - - - - -

_____

5. Fill in the missing letters and say the word:

hide   hid

hid __   hi __

hi __ __   h __ __

h __ __ __   __ __ __

__ __ __ __

Verbs: Section 4
Worksheet 47-2 (hid)

Name: _____ **Date:** _____

6. **Write and say the word four times:**

hide   hid

‾‾‾‾‾‾‾‾‾‾‾‾‾‾‾‾‾‾‾‾‾‾‾   ‾‾‾‾‾‾‾‾‾‾‾‾‾‾‾‾‾‾‾‾‾‾‾
‾ ‾ ‾ ‾ ‾ ‾ ‾ ‾ ‾ ‾ ‾ ‾   ‾ ‾ ‾ ‾ ‾ ‾ ‾ ‾ ‾ ‾ ‾ ‾
‾‾‾‾‾‾‾‾‾‾‾‾‾‾‾‾‾‾‾‾‾‾‾   ‾‾‾‾‾‾‾‾‾‾‾‾‾‾‾‾‾‾‾‾‾‾‾
‾ ‾ ‾ ‾ ‾ ‾ ‾ ‾ ‾ ‾ ‾ ‾   ‾ ‾ ‾ ‾ ‾ ‾ ‾ ‾ ‾ ‾ ‾ ‾
‾‾‾‾‾‾‾‾‾‾‾‾‾‾‾‾‾‾‾‾‾‾‾   ‾‾‾‾‾‾‾‾‾‾‾‾‾‾‾‾‾‾‾‾‾‾‾
‾ ‾ ‾ ‾ ‾ ‾ ‾ ‾ ‾ ‾ ‾ ‾   ‾ ‾ ‾ ‾ ‾ ‾ ‾ ‾ ‾ ‾ ‾ ‾
‾‾‾‾‾‾‾‾‾‾‾‾‾‾‾‾‾‾‾‾‾‾‾   ‾‾‾‾‾‾‾‾‾‾‾‾‾‾‾‾‾‾‾‾‾‾‾

7. **Study the two words below.**
Then close your eyes and spell:

hide

hid

Put a 1 in each little box for your answer.
Add up your answers.
Write the total in this big box.

Verbs: Section 4
Worksheet 47-3 (hid)

Name: _____ **Date:** _____

Color and cut out the tree and the boy.
Make the boy hide behind the tree.

1. What is the boy doing?
2. What did he do?
3. Tell a story about a boy hiding from his sister.

Verbs: Section 4
Activity Sheet 47 (hid)

◯

△

is hanging

hung

1. **Find the picture that matches.**
   Fill in the blank with the correct word:

◯ The rabbit is hanging up the clothes.

△ The rabbit _____ up the clothes.

   hang
   hung

2. **Write and say:**

   is hanging

   hung

   _____

   _____

   _____

   _____

Verbs: Section 4
Worksheet 48-1 (hung)

3. Fill in and say:

We _____ the decorations on the
Christmas tree.

4. Answer the question. Write your sentence in the blank:

Where did you hang your clothes last night?

_____
- -
_____
_____
- -
_____

5. Fill in the missing letters and say the word:

hang	hung
han __	hun __
ha __ __	hu __ __
h __ __ __	h __ __ __
__ __ __ __	__ __ __ __

6. Write and say the word four times:

hang

hung

**7. Study the two words below.
Then close your eyes and spell:**

hang

hung

**Put a 1 in each little box for your answer.
Add up your answers.
Write the total in this big box.**

Verbs: Section 4
Worksheet 48-3 (hung)

Name: _____ **Date:** _____

Draw a picture of yourself.
Hang it on the wall.

1. What did you do?
2. Where did you hang it?

Name: _____ **Date:** _____

Fill in the blank with the correct word.
Then say the complete sentence:

1. Yesterday I _____ the cat.

   am feeding

   fed

2. Now I _____ the picture.

   am hanging

   hung

3. Yesterday he _____ on the ice.

   slide

   slid

4. Now he _____ in my backyard.

   swung

   is swinging

5. Yesterday I _____ from my brother.

   hid

   hide

6. Right now she _____ the cat.

   fed

   is feeding

7. Yesterday I _____ a picture.

   hang

   hung   ☐

8. Now the dog _____ from me.

   hid

   is hiding   ☐

9. Yesterday I _____ all morning.

   am swinging

   swung   ☐

10. Now she _____ on the ice.

   is sliding

   slide   ☐

Put a 1 in each little box for your answer.
Add up your answers.
Write the total in this big box.

Verbs: Section 4
Review 12-2

Picture Summary

Teacher:

On the following page is a picture summary. Look at the picture with the student and discuss what all of the animals are doing. First use the present progressive tense.

is falling
is catching
is throwing
is building
is digging
is flying
is blowing
is swimming
is swinging
is sliding
is hiding
is hanging

Then say, "This picture was taken yesterday. Tell me what each animal did." Encourage the student to use each of the 12 verbs covered in the section in the past tense.

Name: _____   Date: _____

Verbs: Section 4
Picture Summary 4-2

Egg Game

Teacher:
Laminate the baskets and eggs for prolonged use. Cut them out.

1. Give each player a basket.
2. Turn all the eggs face down on the table.
3. The first player chooses an egg. If the egg contains a word, the player uses the word in a sentence. If the sentence is correct, the player places the egg on his or her basket.
4. If the sentence is wrong, the player must put the egg back on the table and the next player takes a turn.
5. If an egg says, "Pick another egg," the player keeps that egg and chooses another one.
6. The player with the most eggs wins.

Verbs: Section 4
Game 5-2

swing

swung

slide

slid

hide

hid

hang

hung

Pick another egg.

Pick another egg.

Pick another egg.

Pick another egg.

Pick another egg.

Pick another egg.

Pick another egg.

Pick another egg.

Verbs: Section 4
Game 5-3

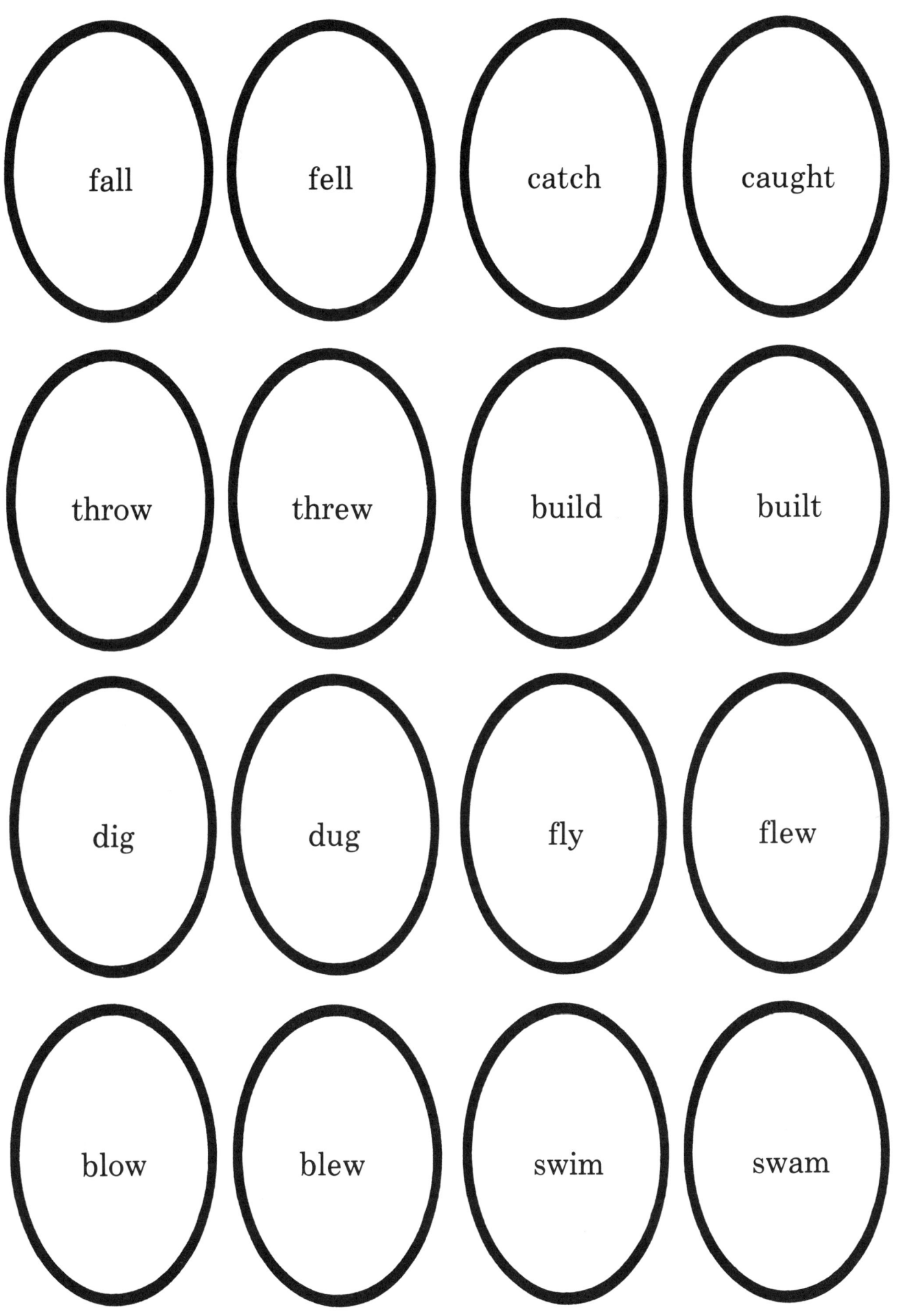

fall   fell   catch   caught

throw   threw   build   built

dig   dug   fly   flew

blow   blew   swim   swam

Verbs: Section 4
Game 5-4

Name: _____ **Date:** _____

Writing Sentences

Write a sentence for each of these words.

1. flew

2. slid

3. threw

4. hung

5. swam

6. dug

Verbs: Section 4
Summary 7-1

7. fell   _____ ☐

8. built   _____ ☐

9. caught _____ ☐

10. hid   _____ ☐

Put a 1 in each little box for your answer.
Add up your answers.
Write the total in this big box.

Verbs: Section 4
Summary 7-2

Word Wheel

1. Cut out the spinner. Attach it to the wheel.
2. Spin the spinner and say the word it stops on.
3. Say the past tense of the word.
4. Use the past tense in a sentence.
5. Put a check in each completed wedge.

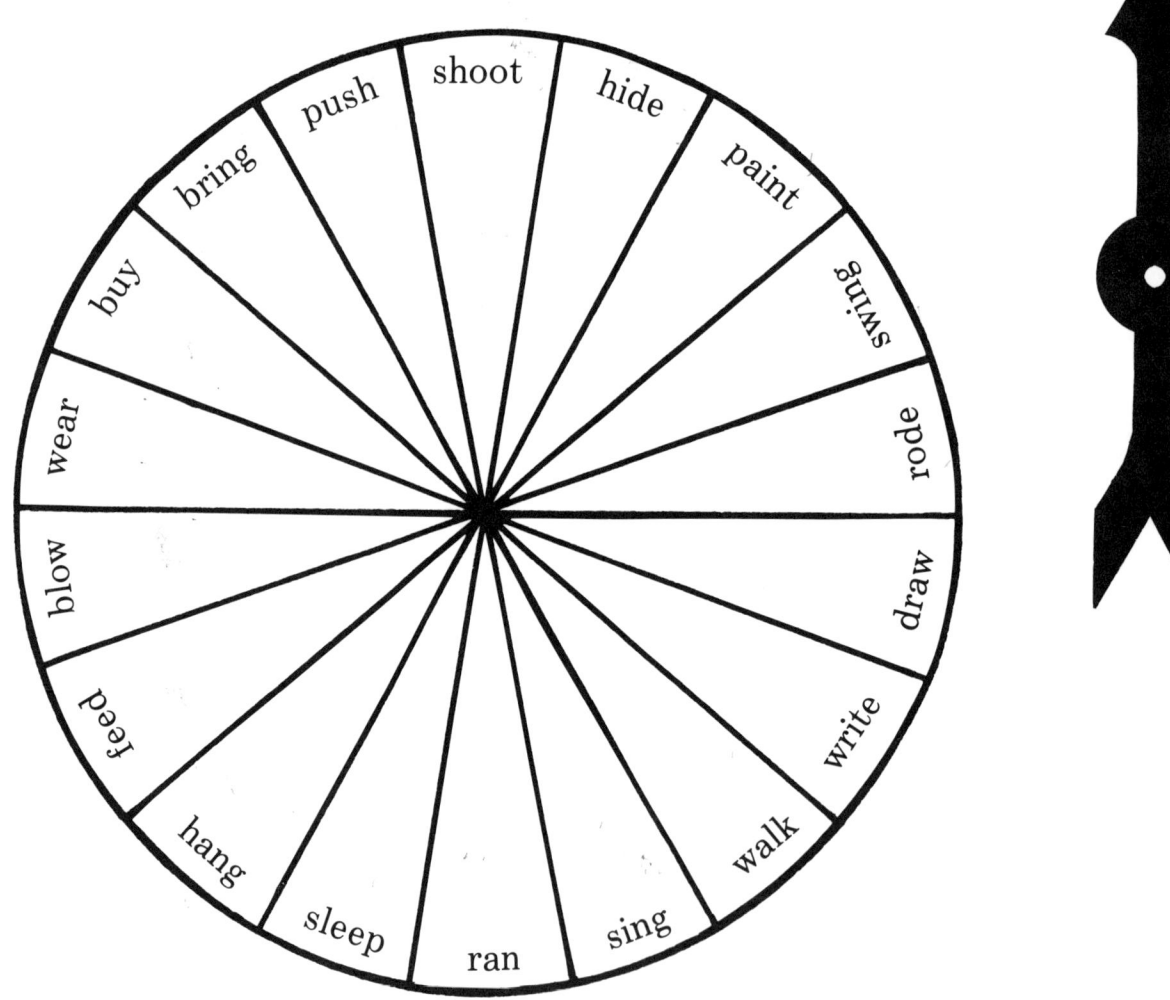

Name: _____

Progress Chart 4

Worksheet Number	Verbs	Date	Questions Completed	Total Possible
37.	fell			7
38.	caught			7
39.	threw			7
40.	built			7
Review 10				10
41.	dug			7
42.	flew			7
43.	blew			7
44.	swam			7
Review 11				10
45.	swung			7
46.	slid			7
47.	hid			7
48.	hung			7
Review 12				10
Summary 7				10
Summary 8				18

Other products from Communication Skill Builders . . .

SHAPE UP YOUR LANGUAGE (1983)　　　*by Joan M. Frazer and Cynthia J. Smith*

You can help your students learn regular and irregular noun, verb, and adjective trans-formations with these high-interest reproducible worksheets and motivating manipula-tives. Three volumes of activities, photocopiable flashcards, and three clear acrylic shapes with picture-and-word strips combine to make a complete program for develop-ing oral and written language.

Shape Up Your Language Complete Program	No. 2071-Y	$99.95
Part I: Verbs – Past Tense	No. 7024-Y	$24.95
Part II: Nouns – Plurals	No. 7025-Y	$24.95
Part III: Adjectives – Comparatives and Superlatives	No. 7026-Y	$24.95

AROUND THE HOME (1982)

Four brightly colored gameboards – with sets of individual object cards – offer an enjoyable new format for language stimulation. Each gameboard shows everyday scenes in the kitchen, garden, workshop, and through the house. Captivating cartoon characters are engaged in common household activities that your students can talk about.　　　**No. 4601-Y　$19.95**

FLIP IT S & Z
FLIP IT R
FLIP IT SH, CH, & J (1983)　　　*by Susan Housel, Debra Polson, and Nancy Herron*

These color cartoon "flip" books offer you an alternative in drill materials. Each book contains nine sound-centered sentences. By flipping through each sectioned book, your students will find a multitude of humorous sentence combinations. Reach articulation and language goals in a new way!

Flip It S & Z	No. 4620-Y	$8.95
Flip It R	No. 4621-Y	$8.95
Flip It SH, CH, & J	No. 4685-Y	$8.95

SPEECH, LANGUAGE, AND READING WORKSHEETS (1983)
by Margaret F. Smith

Eighty-one reproducible pages help you tie in speech-language skills with reading skills to help your students succeed academically. Use these activities to supplement your daily lessons, for class presentations, for individual sessions, and as take-home work.　　　**No. 4636-Y　$21.95**

SOUND INVESTMENTS (1983)　　　*by Elizabeth Wilson*

Twenty units of reproducible activities develop listening skills and involve parents. You can help strengthen your students' auditory perceptual skills – and see their school performance improve with better listening. This new curriculum features 189 reproduc-ible sheets for home and classroom carryover.　　　**No. 2077-Y　$35**

Communication Skill Builders
3130 N. Dodge Blvd. / P.O. Box 42050
Tucson, Arizona 85733
(602) 323-7500

Flashcards

Use the following pages to make flashcards.

Instructions:
1. Reproduce each page, front and back, on card stock. Be sure the back of the reproduced copy matches the front.
2. Cut the cards out on the inside of the black line on the picture side.
3. Laminate the cards for durability.
4. Turn to page 1 for instructions on how to use the cards.

 **is finding**

 **is eating**

 **is sitting**

 **is taking**

Verbs: Section 2
Flashcards

is finding

Verbs 13a

is eating

Verbs 14a

is sitting

Verbs 15a

is taking

Verbs 16a

 found

 ate

 sat

 took

Verbs: Section 2
Flashcards

found

Verbs 13b

ate

Verbs 14b

sat

Verbs 15b

took

Verbs 16b

are breaking

is drinking

is shaking

is wearing

Verbs: Section 2
Flashcards

are breaking

Verbs 17a

is drinking

Verbs 18a

is shaking

Verbs 19a

is wearing

Verbs 20a

broke

drank

shook

wore

Verbs: Section 2
Flashcards

broke

Verbs 17b

drank

Verbs 18b

shook

Verbs 19b

wore

Verbs 20b

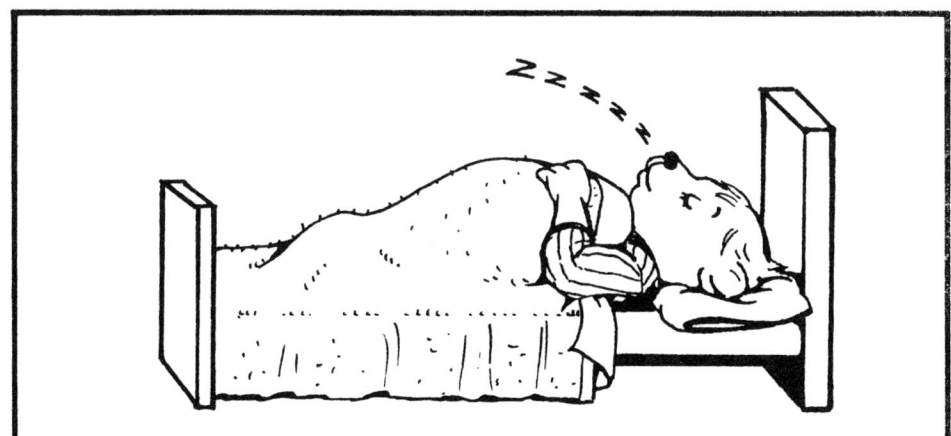

is sleeping

is feeding

is sweeping

is bringing

Verbs: Section 2
Flashcards

is sleeping

Verbs 21a

is feeding

Verbs 22a

is sweeping

Verbs 23a

is bringing

Verbs 24a

slept

fed

swept

brought

Verbs: Section 2
Flashcards

slept

fed

swept

brought

is singing

is studying

is giving

is drawing

Verbs: Section 3
Flashcards

is singing

Verbs 25a

is studying

Verbs 26a

is giving

Verbs 27a

is drawing

Verbs 28a

sang

studied

gave

drew

Verbs: Section 3
Flashcards

sang

Verbs 25b

studied

Verbs 26b

gave

Verbs 27b

drew

Verbs 28b

 is running

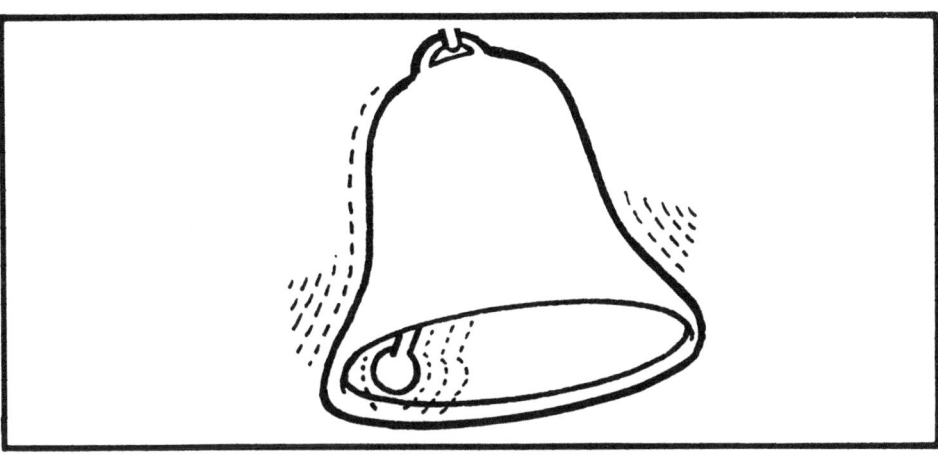 is ringing

 is striking

 is riding

is running

Verbs 29a

is ringing

Verbs 30a

is striking

Verbs 31a

is riding

Verbs 32a

ran

rang

struck

rode

Verbs: Section 3
Flashcards

ran

Verbs 29b

rang

Verbs 30b

struck

Verbs 31b

rode

Verbs 32b

is making

is shooting

is writing

is buying

Verbs: Section 3
Flashcards

is making

Verbs 33a

is shooting

Verbs 34a

is writing

Verbs 35a

is buying

Verbs 36a

made

shot

wrote

bought

Verbs: Section 3
Flashcards

made

Verbs 33b

shot

Verbs 34b

wrote

Verbs 35b

bought

Verbs 36b

is falling

is catching

is throwing

is building

Verbs: Section 4
Flashcards

is falling

Verbs 37a

is catching

Verbs 38a

is throwing

Verbs 39a

is building

Verbs 40a

fell

caught

threw

built

Verbs: Section 4
Flashcards

fell

caught

threw

built

is digging

is flying

is blowing

is swimming

Verbs: Section 4
Flashcards

is digging

Verbs 41a

is flying

Verbs 42a

is blowing

Verbs 43a

is swimming

Verbs 44a

dug

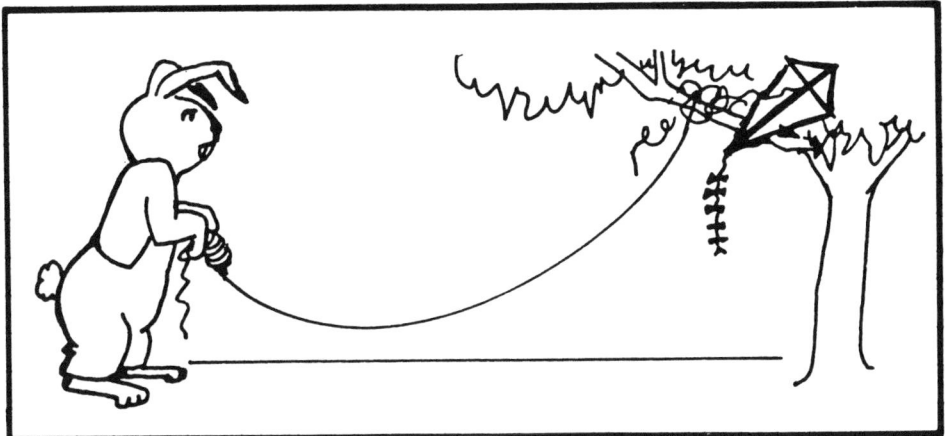

flew

blew

swam

Verbs: Section 4
Flashcards

dug

Verbs 41b

flew

Verbs 42b

blew

Verbs 43b

swam

Verbs 44b

is swinging

is sliding

is hiding

is hanging

Verbs: Section 4
Flashcards

is swinging

Verbs 45a

is sliding

Verbs 46a

is hiding

Verbs 47a

is hanging

Verbs 48a

swung

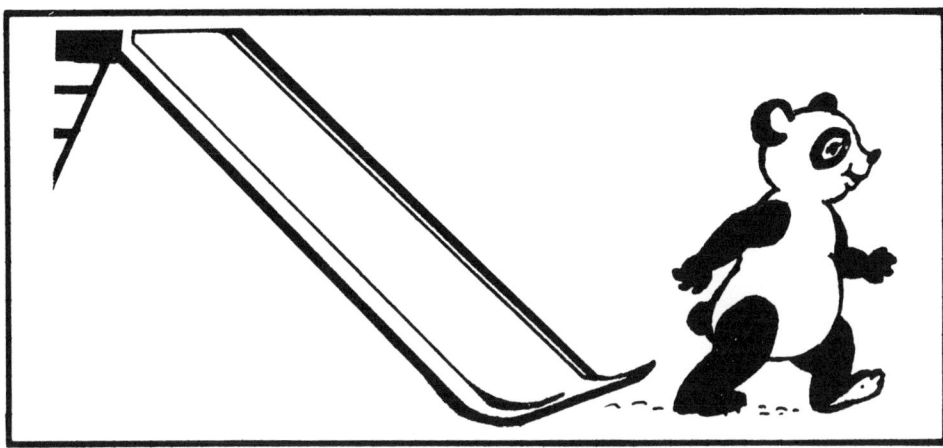

slid

hid

hung

Verbs: Section 4
Flashcards

swung

slid

hid

hung